Unordained Elders
and
Renewal Communities

DEDICATION

To Bishop Alexander Zaleski, for whom this was written, who died before he could read it and

To the communities of Genesee, Mt. Savior and New Melleray, who continue the ancient monastic custom of generous hospitality and who have shared the life of their communities with us

Unordained Elders
and
Renewal Communities

by
Stephen B. Clark

Paulist Press
New York/Paramus/Toronto

Library of Congress
Catalog Card Number: 75-35329

ISBN: 0-8091-1916-1

Published by Paulist Press
Editorial Office: 1865 Broadway, N.Y., N.Y. 10023
Business Office: 400 Sette Drive, Paramus, N.J. 07652

Printed and bound in the
United States of America

Contents

  I Renewal Movements and Renewal Communities................. 7 *– cy. p.8*

 II The Ascetic Movement as Renewal Movement 10

III Unordained Elders in Patristic Tradition............................ 36

 IV Ordination and Renewal Communities............................... 50

  V Renewal Communities Contribute Leaders......................... 61

 VI Conclusion 75

Notes 81

Bibliography.. 95

Acknowledgments

The author would like to express his thanks to all those who assisted in preparing this manuscript, especially Mr. Nicholas S. Cavnar for his significant contributions in both research and editing, and to Fr. Kilian McDonnell, OSB, Fr. George Montague, S.M. and Fr. Paul Lebau S.J. who were generous with their help.

I
Renewal Movements and Renewal Communities

The decade since the opening of the Vatican Council has been a time of major pastoral challenge for the Catholic Church. The Church has seen many and rapid changes, as has society at large, and has realized the need to adapt its pastoral structures to meet the new conditions. One of the greatest of these pastoral challenges is that presented by the charismatic renewal. Like any other rapidly growing popular movement, the charismatic renewal (which perhaps trebles each year) could prove difficult to constructively integrate into the life of the Church. While the growth of the movement has thus far been remarkably positive and little disruptive, a need still exists for solid pastoral consideration of the renewal and its relationship to the Church.

People looking at the charismatic renewal and considering its future frequently express a fear of sectarianism. As the renewal forms and develops, it would seemingly be easy for it to split off from the Catholic Church and go its own way, or perhaps to subtly form into a church within a church or into a gnostic movement for the spiritually elite. Occasionally voices are raised that call to mind Troeltsch's distinction between church and sect,[1] warning that while the Catholic Church has deliberately chosen to be a church, the charismatic renewal is in danger of becoming a sect. Others point to the history of early Methodism, which began as a movement within a church but became a church of its own.

Such warnings usually show insufficient awareness of the difference between Protestant and Catholic history: almost all the ex-

1

amples are drawn from Protestant history. Troeltsch, for instance, developed his types of "church" and "sect" primarily as a means of describing the difference between the German state church and smaller Protestant sects. In fact, from a wider perspective according to his description, we would have to describe the Catholic Church itself as a "sect" in predominantly Protestant countries. Nor is the example of the Methodists completely applicable. The Methodists left the Anglican, not the Roman, Catholic Church.

In Catholic history, on the other hand, many renewal movements have been successfully integrated into the life of the Church, making a significant contribution to the Church as a whole. The ascetic movement of the fourth century is one example, the mendicant movement of the thirteenth another, and there are many more. Catholicism has a pastoral wisdom of its own, a wisdom nowhere more apparent than in an ability to integrate renewal movements rather than force them into separate sects. It has had failures (perhaps its most notable failure was the Protestant movement itself) and, to be sure, there have been successes in Protestant churches, but there is nonetheless an accumulated wisdom belonging to the Catholic tradition which can easily be successful if applied well. In fact, the much more orderly, constructive history of the Catholic charismatic renewal in comparison to the earlier pentecostal movement and the more recent neo-pentecostal developments is in large part due to the instinctive use of that wisdom by both the leaders of the renewal and the hierarchy of the Church.

There has been a variety of movements in the history of Christianity, not all of which were renewal movements. Gnosticism, for instance, was more a syncretistic movement than a renewal movement. It reinterpreted Christian doctrinal statements and Christian practice in a way that permitted the amalgamation of some very foreign religious elements. Arianism was a (heretical) movement for doctrinal reform rather than for renewal. The term "renewal movement" is here applied to those movements in which the central thrust is towards a more fervent and effective living of the Christian life. Most renewal movements also pick up other concerns as they develop, but their essential characteristic is a focus on the renewal of basic Christian living. Besides the ascetic movement of the fourth century and the movement associated with Innocent III and the mendicant orders in the twelfth and thirteenth centuries, historic renewal movements include the movement begun by the Cluniac reformers in the eleventh century, the evangelical movement among Protestants in the eighteenth and nineteenth centuries, and the "Oxford Movement" among Anglicans and Catholics in the nineteenth century.[2] Such movements usually arise when the life of the Church has been weakened by either changes in society or changes in the Church or by both. They are the instinctive response of Christians who wish to restore Christian living to vitality despite the erosion of social change.[3]

Renewal movements are a positive and constructive force in the life of the Church, but by their very nature they present a special pastoral challenge. They touch, especially in their early stages, only some Christians, and the "renewed Christians" and the "unrenewed Christians" must then live together. Elitism, divisiveness, and similar problems can result. The need arises to find a way for those who are part of the renewal movement to live in the Church and relate to others in the Church constructively. That pastoral challenge presented by any renewal movement is precisely the challenge the charismatic renewal presents to the Church today.

Much "traditional wisdom" has already been used to integrate the Catholic charismatic renewal into the life of the Catholic Church. The structures which have served to relate such movements as the third orders, the Christian Family Movement, and the Cursillo Movement have all been successfully employed. Three pastoral devices have proven particularly helpful. The first is the structure of a parish organization with a priest as chaplain. Although most charismatic prayer groups are not formally considered parish organizations, many relate to parishes in just that way. (Here we must bear in mind that the priest-chaplain participates in most parish organizations only at crisis moments and solemn ceremonial occasions.) The second is the appointment of a bishop's representative to the diocesan-wide renewal movement (or renewal center), a model which has been used for many lay movements in this century and is again being used successfully for the charismatic renewal. The third is active participation of many priests in the renewal movement, both as leaders and simply as participants. As long as ordained leaders of the Church are part of the movement, they will provide an effective, if informal, bond between it and the Church as a whole.

However, a further level of need for integration is appearing. As the charismatic movement grows, more developed forms are appearing, forms which are highly structured and often very effective. This is happening for several reasons: the leadership of the charismatic renewal wants to be responsible and see the movement conducted in an orderly, constructive way and consequently form more ordered, committed bodies; the Church as a whole is not ready to adopt the renewal, and so the renewal must develop within specifically charismatic groupings; those involved in the renewal want to make positive contributions to the work of the Church and therefore organize to do so. Perhaps the most common form groups in the charismatic renewal are taking is the charismatic community. These communities are developing a new form of Christian life and service based upon the charismatic renewal.

Communities like the new charismatic communities have been common throughout the history of the Church. As renewal movements have appeared and grown, the people involved have collected to form communities within the Church where they could live a life permeated by the movements' ideals—renewal communities. The ascetic movement produced the earliest monasteries and convents; the mendicant movement produced the great religious orders of Franciscans and Dominicans. Today, renewal communities are developing not only within the charismatic renewal,[4] but also as part of the movement of *communidades de base* in the Latin countries of Europe and America. It seems to be almost a sociological law: renewal movements produce renewal communities.

The integration of renewal communities into the life of the wider Church presents a special pastoral challenge. First of all, the communities have a developed life together. Their members do more than just come together for meetings. They care for one another personally; they share their financial and material resources; they develop patterns of life that are significantly different from those around them. In order for their life together as a community to go well, they need an authority of their own that does more than simply organize and preside over certain meetings and activities. They need an authority that is able to take a directive role in people's lives. However, for such an authority to exist in a healthy way in the life of the Church, it should be related to the authority structures of the wider Church in some ongoing way.

Renewal communities also present a special pastoral challenge because they are usually more united as a group of people than the local parish(es). The church is thus faced with a bloc, a cohesive group within the parish or diocese that cannot be treated merely as individual members of the church, but must also be dealt with as a group. And they must be dealt with through leaders who are not necessarily official leaders of the church. In other words, the renewal community presents a relationship problem—the problem of relating one group of people, a community, to another group of people, the Church as a whole. The relationship is complicated by the fact that the two groups are not separate (like two churches) but one belongs to the other. If this relationship is not worked out well, the existence of the renewal community could harm rather than strengthen the life of the Church.

One solution to this pastoral difficulty is to have the renewal community simply take over one of the normal subgroupings of the official Church structure, becoming a parish or diocese within the Church. Such an option has been successfully tried. The Episcopal Church of the Redeemer in Houston is one example of a parish which became a charismatic community,[5] and there are others. That is, in fact, an ancient solution. Many monastic establishments of the Middle Ages were for all practical purposes parishes within their dioceses; in the Celtic Church of late antiquity, in fact, they were often the equivalent of dioceses. But that option is not likely to become prevalent. It works best in situations where the original parish is dead or dying, or in missionary situations where the parish system does not yet exist. In situations where a large body of Christians has no intention of becoming part of the renewal community (as will probably be the case in most Catholic parishes for a while to come), a different solution is needed.

The solution for most situations lies in establishing a good relationship between the emerging renewal communities and the official leadership of the Church. The proper structure for that relationship and the right principles for conducting it must be discovered. Here a look at a historic renewal movement which was successfully and constructively integrated into the Church can be helpful.

The ascetic movement[6] of the fourth century makes a particularly valuable subject for such a study. For one thing, it holds an honored place in Catholic tradition. As a movement, it has been accepted as an authentic voice within the Church; it has, in effect, been "canonized." Not only do ascetic communities hold a recognized position in the order of the Catholic Church, but the ascetic life and approach to Christianity is explicitly honored in the Church's spiritual teaching. The prominent figures of the movement have become the most honored saints and doctors of Christianity: Basil, Augustine, Jerome, John Chrysostom, Gregory of Nazianzus, and Gregory the Great are only a few of the greatest. In short, the ascetic movement is a "safe" example to use:[7] it is widely acknowledged as the model of a renewal movement making a valuable contribution to the Church.

There is, however, an even better reason to choose the ascetic movement for this particular study: it was, at least in its earliest period, a movement very similar to the charismatic renewal. It too rose in an era when the Church was subject to major social change. It too began among people who were predominantly laymen and spread rapidly as an unorganized movement that reached to all parts of the Church. Florovsky states:

> "Monks were leaving the world to build, on the virginal soil of the desert, a new society; to organize there, on the evangelical pattern, the true Christian community. Early monasticism was not an ecclesiastical institution. It was precisely a spontaneous movement, a drive. And it was distinctively a lay movement."[8]

A pastoral study of the ascetic movement can uncover the pastoral-theological principles used in resolving the challenges that renewal presented to the fourth-century Church. Very few studies of the ascetic movement have been made from a primarily pastoral perspective.[9] Most consider it from the viewpoint of spirituality or ideology, with a primary interest in the doctrine or way of life of the early ascetics. Those concerned with the structural and leadership patterns discussed in this study usually take a sacramental perspective. While such sacramental studies contribute to an understanding of the pastoral realities, they rarely treat fully or explicitly the way different structural and leadership arrangements functioned in the life of a people (what they did or did not accomplish).[10] For instance, a medieval chantry priest and the pastor of a parish both fulfill the sacramental definition of priest, which is usually framed in terms of the priest's relationship to the sacraments or the bishop. Yet functionally (pastorally) they are quite different. Once the pastoral perspective becomes primary, the significance of the pastoral strategy of the fourth-century bishops in regard to the ascetic movement becomes easier to see.

Ordination will be a central concern in this study, because ordination was the key in the development of the pastoral structures that integrated the ascetic movement into the Church as a whole. From the pastoral point of view (prescinding from the sacramental perspective), ordination is the ordering of leadership (headship) relations. Ordained bishops and priests are not the only Christian heads[11] or "pastors."[12] The father of a family, for instance, fulfills this function. Nor are the bishops and priests the only Christian leaders. They are, however, the officially recognized heads and can act on behalf of the Church as a body: ordination is the regularizing (formalization) of their headship over the Church as a whole.[13] Pastorally speaking, it is appropriate, in fact necessary, that the heads of the Church have such sacramental powers as the power to preside at the eucharistic assemblies, the power to initiate people into the Church, and the power to discipline. But for the purposes of this study, the most important characteristic of ordination is its role in establishing the official heads of the church body.

The question facing the Church today is: how should a renewal community be integrated into the life of the Church as a whole so that it can contribute to the building up and strengthening of that life (how should it be integrated pastorally?), and therefore, how should its leadership be related to the official Church leadership? A study of the ascetic movement in the patristic era yields the following principles as elements of a successful solution:

(1) The unordained elder is an important figure within the tradition of the Church, not an abuse: having unordained elders allows pastoral flexibility and innovation, especially in a new or changing situation.

(2) The normal way for a renewal community to be related to the Church as a whole is by the ordination of its leader(s) to the presbyterate of the diocese in which the community is situated.

(3) The renewal community should be drawn upon to make an important contribution to the pastoral strength and the ordained leadership of the Church as a whole.

Before considering these principles, we need a further examination of the ascetic movement itself, focusing on its nature as a movement of renewal and on the comparison it offers to the charismatic renewal. An examination of the development of ascetic renewal communities and a description of the social forms those communities took will then complete the background necessary to understanding the way the fourth-century bishops and the ascetic leaders used the above principles in successfully and constructively integrating the movement into the life of the Church.

II
The Ascetic Movement as Renewal Movement

A comparison of early asceticism and the charismatic renewal may not seem obvious at first. While many people are acquainted with the history of the fourth and fifth century ascetics, they are not familiar with the idea of an "ascetic movement" as a renewal movement similar to the charismatic renewal. There are several reasons for that unfamiliarity. For one thing, few people are accustomed to thinking of historical movements in terms of patterns of social relationships. Without sociological training, they do not naturally think in terms of organized and unorganized movements and eras of major social change. Nor are most histories of the ascetic movement written in those terms; for the most part, those studying early asceticism have other interests than its dynamics as a movement. Hence the similarities with the charismatic renewal that do exist are often overlooked.

Another reason people fail to recognize those similarities is that they view the ascetic movement primarily in terms of its later forms. Since the middle ages, monasticism in the western Church has been highly institutionalized, clericalized, and tightly integrated into the structures of the Church. It is scarcely a spontaneous, popular movement. The beginnings of the ascetic movement were, however, quite different, and it is in those beginnings that we can trace the outlines of a social and religious phenomenon very similar to the charismatic renewal. For the purposes of this study, we define the "early ascetic movement" as the period from Anthony of Egypt's appearance as an ascetic teacher (c. 305 A.D.) to the

Council of Chalcedon (451 A.D.). A few examples are drawn from periods later than 451, but in general that date marks the end of the study. In this period, asceticism emerged as a renewal movement and found a structural relationship with the Church as a whole which it still maintains in the Eastern Church.[14] In the West, that relationship was not replaced until the rise of exemption and religious orders in the tenth and eleventh centuries.

One final reason people overlook the similarities between the ascetic movement and the charismatic renewal is the influence of various forms of scholarship unsympathetic to asceticism or to the institutional Catholic Church. Many scholars (even some Catholics among them nowadays) prefer to see the ascetic movement as a primarily non-Christian influence upon Christianity—a form of Manicheanism, or neo-Platonism, or Christianized Greek "philosophy." Or they set up strong contrasts between spirit and institution, charismatic authority and hierarchical authority, popular movement and official structure.[15] Such approaches block an objective appraisal of asceticism as a movement of Christian renewal. At the same time much of the modern Christian scholarship which approaches both the early ascetic movement and the Church institution sympathetically and which increasingly understands the movement as a renewal is as yet unfamiliar to people outside the field.[16]

In fact, despite unfamiliarity with the idea, the early ascetic movement was very much like the charismatic renewal in its social structures. That can be shown through consideration of the development and nature of the ascetic movement as a broad popular movement and consideration of the goals the ascetics themselves had in the movement as a renewal. In this context is is possible to see how the renewal communities developed precisely as an attempt to recover the basics of Christian living.

The Movement

In 305 A.D., Anthony of Egypt emerged victorious from twenty years of ascetic withdrawal and combat with demons in an abandoned fort on the southern Nile. In that year, he began to attract men who became his disciples and who carried the way of life he exemplified on to other places. Hilarion, for example, one of the first of those men, returned to his native Palestine as early as 308 to live as an ascetic in the desert near Gaza and from his influence the ascetic movement began to grow in Palestine. Shortly after Anthony's emergence, a young man named Pachomius was converted in another Egyptian village and attached himself to an ascetic master named Palamon. In 320, after hearing God's call to establish a community of ascetics, he moved to the abandoned village of Tabenna where he founded the first recognized coeno-bium. From Tabenna a network of coenobia, organized much like a religious order, soon spread across Egypt. During the next twenty years other ascetic settlements appeared, frequently under no traceable influence from Anthony or Pachomius: on the mountain of Nitria by 325, in the desert of Scete by 330, in the cities of Oxyrhyncus and Arsinoe by 340. Within 35 years of Anthony's emergence at Pispir, coenobia and eremetic settlements filled Egypt and were attracting thousands of Egyptian Christians.[17] A broad-based, popular movement had appeared that has since been recognized by historians and theologians as a well-defined, unified movement within Christianity: the ascetic movement.[18]

Egypt has been justly considered the cradle of that movement. The lives and teachings of the Egyptian fathers provided the primary example and impetus in the spread of the ascetic movement to other countries. Yet evidence discovered in recent years points to an independent development in some other countries.[19] Syrian monasticism grew up on its own at about the same time and speed as Egyptian.[20] Palestine quite possibly had independent origins from early in the fourth century.[21] In Asia Minor, an ascetic movement associated with Eustathius of Sebaste rose in the third decade of the century which cannot be traced with certainty to either Egyptian or Syrian influence.[22] Eustathius and his disciples played an important part in the ascetic development of Basil the Great.

Whatever its actual lineage in each country, by the end of the fourth century the ascetic movement was spreading rapidly throughout the Christian world, especially in the countries of the eastern Mediterranean.[23] Egyptian ascetics had settled in every part of their own country. Their influence (accompanied to some extent by Syrian influence) was extending into Palestine, where the Holy Places attracted increasing numbers of devout Christians. By the beginning of the fifth century, Palestine was well on its way to becoming the great center of ascetic life which it was up to and even after the Islamic conquest. In Syria as in Egypt, ascetics were to be found in every part of the country, and their numbers were very large. Moreover, the Syrian movement reached east beyond the borders of Rome into the Sassanid Empire and north into Armenia and Georgia. Ascetic settlements dotted much of Asia Minor, where the movement had received a great impetus from Basil after his tour of the East in 358. Developments in the Aegean were somewhat slower, but well underway by the beginning of the fifth century. During the same period Constantinople was attracting the first of those monks who, in the course of that century, became so influential in its history.

The ascetic movement spread somewhat more slowly in the West.[24] Athanasius, while on his journeys in exile, apparently encouraged the first growths of the movement in Italy and at Treves. During their exiles, Hilary of Poitiers and Eusebius of Vercelli made direct contact with the movement in the East. Martin of Tours, who contacted the movement in northern Italy before 360, had a major role in introducing it to Gaul.

By the end of the century, with the help of further contacts with the East, the ascetic movement was well underway in most of the western Empire. It penetrated Spain by 380, and established itself in Africa even before Augustine's return in 388. Augustine gave it a significant impetus, so that by the time of the Vandal invasion there were thousands of ascetics throughout northern Africa. In Gaul, the movement experienced major growth at the turn of the fourth century through the influence of Martin's disciples and a number of prominent *conversi*, including Paulinus of Nola

and Sulpicius Severus. Cassian's arrival at Marseilles and the
emergence of Honoratus at Lerins at the beginning of the fifth century sparked a rapid growth of the movement in southern Gaul,
and from there throughout and later beyond Gaul. While Italy was
perhaps slower, monasteries could be found in the major cities
before the fifth century, and the movement continued to grow. In
short, by the time of the Council of Chalcedon the ascetic movement had touched almost every part of the western Christian world
and involved thousands of Christians.

The ascetic movement did more than increase in numbers and
spread geographically. By the first decades of the fifth century it
had achieved a very prestigious position in the Church. That position was strongest in Egypt and Syria, and only later reached the
same proportions at the peripheries of the Christian world. But by
the time of Chalcedon, the ascetic movement was clearly recognized as an integrated and accepted part of Christian life and of
the pastoral structure of the Christian people. Not only were
abbots invited to join the bishops at Chalcedon and to sign the
decrees of the council as recognized Christian leaders,[25] but canons
were passed to regulate the place of monastic life in the Church.[26]

We can easily underestimate how extraordinary it was that
the ascetic movement achieved such recognition and acceptance. It
seems today that acceptance would have been a matter of course;
that again stems from thinking of the movement only in its more
"domesticated" forms—the monks of modern religious orders or
the more urbane early representatives like Basil, Augustine, and
Gregory the Great. The movement's contemporaries saw something quite different: the ascetic movement in its beginnings was
often extremist, somewhat disorderly, and contained elements far
more questionable from the viewpoint of traditional Christianity
than anything in today's charismatic renewal. A more complete
picture emerges from the stories of the wandering Syrian monks,
who lived in the mountains and hills almost like wild animals, or
the emaciated ascetics of the Egyptian desert, who vied with one
another in the length and severity of their penances.[27] Moreover,

the ascetics often turned out to be a significant pastoral problem: chapter 1 of the rule of Benedict gives some hint of the problems; Cassian's attempt to deal with the situation illustrates them even more clearly;[28] and some of Palladius' stories are graphic.[29] Finally, the type of asceticism practiced within the movement was very distinctive, and its teachings on spirituality and on interpersonal relationships were highly innovative (these very points have become controversial again in our own day).[30] The ascetic movement was, at times, one of the more extremist, more innovative, more disorderly movements in Christian history, yet it managed to become one of the more constructive; best integrated renewals of the Christian Church.

It is far easier to give an external description of the ascetic movement than to describe or define its inner characteristics. Everyone recognizes that there was such a movement in the fourth century. Most people will agree on how it spread and who was involved. Yet it is difficult to describe exactly what the movement was and even more difficult to formulate a definition or clarifying description. The element that was clearly central to the whole movement was its concern with God himself. The ascetics of the fourth and fifth centuries were earnest about seeking God and about living lives as completely centered upon him as possible. There were, of course, those whose lives were not centered upon God, but they were clearly recognized as poor or hypocritical ascetics: they were not developing an acceptable variant of the movement. God-centeredness—the focus on prayer and worship and love of the creator, the willingness to give up other things to find God more fully—is the structural center out of which the other elements of the ascetic movement can be understood.

However, a great earnestness about God is characteristic of other movements in Christian history. What made the ascetic movement so noticeable was the radical social separation between those who were involved in the movement and other Christians. In reference to this separation, the ascetics were often termed renouncers *(apotaktikoi, renunciantes)* or withdrawers (anchorites).

The ascetic had given up normal life (what he termed the "world"). He had left his family and usually his native district; he had given up much of the social customs and culture of his people. He lived in special groupings among other ascetics or lived by himself so that his contacts with ordinary Christians were very limited. His clothing, his appearance, his way of speaking and relating to other people were so different that he could be instantly recognized. In short, the ascetic movement produced a distinct and conspicuous supra-national counter-culture. Moreover, this social separation was not an accidental feature or by-product of the movement: the early ascetics considered it integral to following Christ and leaving the world. "Renouncing the world" for the ascetic life was the requirement for anyone to be numbered among the ascetics.[31]

Finally, participation in the ascetic movement involved a number of practices which trained or prepared a person to live a more God-centered life. Some of these practices were expressed outwardly: fasting, vigils, silence, regular prayer and spiritual reading, solitude, poverty, obedience, and an ordered pattern of life. Some were more inward and involved a discipline of thoughts and practices of prayer and meditation as well as the development of virtues like patience and humility. Taken all together, these practices added up to a highly disciplined pattern of life so distinctive that the movement is often named "the ascetic movement" in reference to those practices of "asceticism," that is, spiritual "training."

Three elements have been picked out for the clarifying description of the movement: God-centeredness, radical social separation, and ascetic practices.[32] The order and grouping are important. God-centeredness comes first because everything else in the ascetic life had significance for the ascetic only as it helped him to center on God. Because modern authors notice most the distinctive features of the movement, they tend to focus on the ascetic practices or the social separation in defining the movement. But in concentrating on special practices they distort the very life of the movement and miss its significance for men of both that day and this.

"Radical social separation," is a term more sociologically descriptive than the usual possibilities—"absolute renunciation," "separation from the world,"[33] etc. Such a term puts that characteristic of the movement into clearer perspective. The ascetics' decision to separate themselves totally from normal society did not normally spring from negativity towards matter or creation, but from their desire to focus completely on God. Social separation enabled them to avoid circumstances which would make that focus more difficult to maintain; it was a tool, a strategy, for achieving a certain end. The term also underlines a point of great significance for this study: those who were part of the ascetic movement structured themselves into very distinct social units clearly separated from the normal life of the Church even when in close geographical proximity to normal congregations. And this radical social separation was accepted by the Church as a whole.

One further observation will help to clarify the meaning of the term "ascetic movement." It seems intuitively correct to date a distinctive ascetic movement from the emergence of Anthony in 305. Yet after looking more closely at the history of asceticism in the Christian Church, we might well wonder whether Anthony did mark a significantly new development. Before 305 there were many ascetics, especially in the villages of Egypt and Syria, whose lives incorporated all the elements of the above definition of the ascetic movement.[34] They were centered on God exactly as the later ascetics were; they practiced the same radical social separation and the same asceticisms. For example, a group of men and women with a recognized rank in the Syrian church—"the sons and daughters of the covenant" (*benai* and *benat qeiama*)—lived a life very similar to that found in the later ascetic movement. Anthony and Pachomius themselves were trained in the ascetic discipline by well-formed masters who considered it an ancient tradition of the

Church. These masters apparently gave even the ascetic habit, the *schema*, to those we now consider the originators of the movement![35]

There is, however, a reason for placing the beginning of the ascetic movement in 305. From that year on those following the ascetic way of life took on more and more of the characteristics of a social movement.[36] They grew rapidly and spontaneously and were recognized as a new phenomenon. But also, there were two significant developments taking place around 305 that shaped that new movement: the acceptance of the eremetic life, as practiced by Anthony, and the acceptance of the coenobitic life established by Pachomius as the two most normal forms of ascetic life. Both developments meant that ascetics lived in more radical separation from other Christians and in greater unity with one another. Those developments, therefore, contributed to the emergence of a recognizable ascetic movement.[37] In short, something significantly new did indeed happen in the first two decades of the fourth century: out of a long-standing ascetic tradition emerged a distinct social movement that was to have a revolutionary impact on Christianity.

A Renewal Movement

Besides failing to recognize the ascetic movement as a spontaneous popular movement, modern observers also tend to view it as a movement pursuing not a renewal of basic Christian living, but a special form of Christianity. The reason is, again, the tendency for many to read back into the early movement their attitudes and approach towards modern monasticism. Today, we consider the ascetic life something intended for special people, those who have the gift to not marry and who want a more contemplative, ordered, and restrictive life. Monasteries and religious orders exist for these people with a special call; those without that call can live normal lives without feeling they are less fervent Christians. But the early ascetics looked at themselves quite differently. They did not believe they were establishing a special way of life: they felt they were recapturing authentic Christianity in its primitive fervor. They considered their choice the better way, not obligatory for all Christians to be sure, but at least the choice anyone desiring a dedicated Christian life would want to make. Their goal was the renewal of basic Christian life.

Many Catholic scholars have emphasized precisely that point in recent years: the original concept of the monastic life was not of a special way of life, but of Christianity lived to its logical consequences. G. M. Columbas, in an article titled "The Ancient Concept of Monastic Life," puts it this way:

"The monastic life is conceived as the practical realization of the baptismal promises . . . In a word, we see the monk as the authentic Christian who lives the mystery of Christianity in its integrity, to its ultimate consequences."[38]

Armand Veilleux, speaking of Pachomius in "The Abbatial Office in Coenobitic Life," says:

". . . for Pachomius, the life of the monk is the natural outcome of his baptism. The vocation to the koinonia is the complete carrying out of one's baptismal promises."[39]

According to Peter Munz in his article "John Cassian," Cassian

". . . did not think of monasticism as an extraordinary movement and of the life it enjoined as one of the many possible Christian lives. He thought of it as the Christian life *par excellence*: and he must have believed that to a real Christian there was no alternative."[40]

"It is necessary to stress all this in order to show that to Cassian, the desert ascetics were just ordinary spiritual Christians, working for the salvation of their souls."[41]

John Chrysostom himself equated the monastic life with the life of the gospel in *Contra oppugnatores vitae monasticae*:

> "In the Bible, there is no mention of monk or layman. It is men who distinguish the two . . . indeed, the gospels desire all, even the married, to live as monks."[42]

Basil adopted the same approach in his discussions of the ascetic life. He launches the *Long Rules*, his most systematic treatment of the "monastic" life, by presenting the two great commandments— love of God and of neighbor. The ascetic life itself he introduces in a section titled simply "On avoiding distraction" which stresses the importance of a strictly disciplined life in attaining those basic goals every Christian should seek.[43] His ascetic discourses reiterate that view: the same commandments are for everyone, but those who want to follow them more effectively should live the ascetic life.

The way many ascetic fathers received their "call" to ascetic life demonstrates the same basic understanding. Anthony heard the gospel call to discipleship: "If you would be perfect, go and sell all that you have and give to the poor; and come follow me."[44] He responded to that passage by leaving his home to adopt the ascetic life. Arsenius, tutor to the future emperors Arcadius and Honorius, prayed, "Lord, show me the way to salvation." He was told: "Be solitary, be silent, be at rest. These are the roots of a life without sin."[45] Pachomius, after several years of ascetic life, while keeping vigil to learn the perfect will of God for his life, was told in a vision that: "The will of God is to serve the race of men, to reconcile them to him." He immediately set out to found his first coenobium.[46] In all these instances, there was no call to a special way of life: the call was to simple, basic Christian goals—to be a disciple, to find salvation, to overcome sin, to provide reconciliation between God and man. These men responded to that call by dedicating themselves to the ascetic life.

Some of the terminology the early ascetics used also underlines their concern with the renewal of basic Christian living. They encountered a standard difficulty of renewal movements: in attempting to describe the difference between an ascetic and another Christian, they were forced to adopt terms drawn from the process of Christian conversion and initiation. For instance, most of them described the change that made someone an ascetic as "renouncing the world." Now, the "world" most of them were leaving was not usually paganism, but a less fervent form of Christianity. Most were leaving Christian families, in fact, Christian church life in normal parishes, to become monks. Yet they described that life with the term earlier Christians had applied to paganism—"the world." The old contrast between the Christian community and a pagan society became in ascetic writings a contrast between the ascetic community and ordinary life as lived by Christians and pagans alike.

A direct parallel to the use of the term "renouncing the world" in the ascetic movement is the use of the term "baptized in the Spirit" in the charismatic renewal. Being "baptized in the Spirit" is used to describe the experience of spiritual renewal which people find in the charismatic movement. Yet it is also a scriptural term, applied in the New Testament to something happening to a convert at the beginning of his Christian life, not to an experience occuring after a period of time lived as a Christian.[47] Those involved in the charismatic renewal use the term "baptized in the Spirit" because they believe their experience should be a part of basic Christian experience, just as the early ascetics believed their renunciation of the world recaptured an integral part of basic Christian experience. There are many other parallels in Christian history: the use of "conversion" in several Catholic and Protestant renewal movements, the use of "saved" among Evangelicals, the use of "acquire the Spirit" in several Christian groups from the fourth century on.

The point is not that the early ascetics were wrong in using such terminology (although it does become awkward, especially when diocesan priests and the bishop must be described as "worldly" (secular) clergy because they were not living a regular or monastic life). Rather, the point is that they were running up against a classic problem all renewal movements face: how does one talk about the Christianity existing as a result of the renewal movement and about the ordinary Christianity of the majority of Christians? If a person believes he is part of a true renewal movement, i.e., a revival of basic Christianity, he will want to use basic Christian terms to describe what has happened to him. He will want to understand his own Christian renewal as simply a rediscovery of Christianity, or of Christ, or of Christian living. But that often forces him to describe other Christians in terms which, at least on the surface, seem to imply they are *not* Christians at all. The problem is, in fact, unavoidable, because "unrenewed" Christianity is usually missing something basic to Christian living (although it is not usually true that essential Christianity is missing).

As the ascetic movement developed, other theories of the difference between those involved in the movement and ordinary Christians evolved. One commonly used distinction was that of the righteous and the perfect.[48] Ordinary Christians were described as the "righteous" if they kept the basic commandments and lived an acceptable Christian life. Those who became ascetics were described as the "perfect," not meaning that they were flawless, but that they were trying to live the gospel perfection ("If you would be *perfect*, go and sell all that you have and come follow me"). Later on the theory of different calls appeared. Clearly, not everyone could live the ascetic life, giving up marriage and living in total poverty. Moreover, ordinary life had to be maintained for a number of good Christian reasons. Therefore, some people were "called" to an ascetic life, others were not. A discussion of those different approaches is not necessary here; it is only important to note that they were later developments. The primitive approach of the early ascetics was simply to equate their way of life with Christianity (what we might call "renewed Christianity").

Twentieth century Christians often have difficulty believing that the ascetics presented their way of life as a model for normal

Christianity because of the absence of any "apostolic service" in that life. The ascetics used their time in prayer, eating and sleeping, in manual labor: none of it was set apart for the Christian service which modern devout laymen usually finds time for. The ordinary monk played very little part in the evangelization, social action, and works of mercy that many lay societies today engage in. However, the objection again rises from thinking in modern terms. "Apostolic service" as practiced today was not performed by the average fourth century Christian. Most Christians did not undertake to sign up for jobs that would directly build up the Church in a pastoral or evangelistic way. Instead, special individuals, and usually only a few, were chosen for those jobs by the church leaders. The normal Christian would be expected to build up the Church by brotherly love and by working in order to provide for others. The monks performed these services as much as, if not more than, ordinary Christians. The ascetic, in other words, generally lived the life of a devout layman, unless he happened to have the kind of prominence that attracted people looking for the help of a holy man or was called by popular acclaim or by the authorities of the Church to a pastoral or evangelistic service.

Twentieth century Christians also have difficulty believing that the ascetics presented their way of life as a model for normal Christianity because of some of the practices they recommended. Few Christians nowadays would accept silence, a prohibition on laughter, radical social separation, celibacy or a strictly disciplined life (to mention only a few elements) as normative or even recommended for the average Christian. Many Christians would accept those practices as acceptable or even beneficial for certain purposes (living a contemplative life, for instance). But most look at them as special practices, not the model for all fervent Christians. Hence the ascetic movement must have been a special movement. We are not called upon here to evaluate the claims of the ascetic movement or the merits of its teaching or approach to the Christian life. We simply have to observe that viewing the ascetic movement as special can come from an evaluation that many Christians today instinctively make about the recommended practices of the ascetic movement. The early ascetics viewed their way of life differently, and it was easy for them to look at the ascetic life as simply renewed Christianity.

Renewal Communities

Very early in the ascetic movement special renewal communities developed. In order to live according to the ideals of the movement, ascetics grouped themselves into bodies separate from other Christians with systems of authority distinct from the normal pastoral system of the Church. The earliest clear example of such an ascetic renewal community is the coenobium at Tabenna founded in 320. By 451 such communities existed throughout the Christian world.

As in so many other things, the early ascetics did not feel they were doing something new in establishing their communities. They were simply returning to what they viewed as a practice integral to Christianity, clearly taught by the early Church, which needed some revival. In this case, they believed they were returning to the original community life of the first Christians in Jerusalem. Pachomius, his first biographer tells us, fixed his sight from the very first on the "perfect community described in Acts: one heart and one soul."[49] That same example inspired Basil, who said in his *Long Rules*:

"This kind of life has as its aim the glory of God according to the command of our Lord Jesus Christ, who said: 'So let your light shine before men that they may see your good works and glorify your father who is in heaven.' It maintains also the practice characteristic of the saints, of whom it is recorded in Acts: 'And all they that believed were together and had all things in common,' and again: 'And the multitude of believers had but one heart and one soul; neither did anyone say any of the things he possessed was his own, but all things were in common.' "[50]

Jerome said of communal living simply that "The earliest members of the Christian Church lived in the way in which the monks of today try earnestly to live." Augustine felt the same: in a sermon dealing with a crisis in his own household's practice of communal possessions, he referred to their practice as being that of the early Christians.[51] In another sermon, on Psalm 133, he described the first verse—"Behold how good it is and how pleasant, to live as one like brothers"—as having begotten the first monks. The early Christians in Jerusalem were the first to hear that refrain, he said, and the monks were their successors.[52] Cassian believed that the life of the early Christians had never been lost, but had been handed down to the monks, who were now reviving it. In the *Institutes*, he says:

"For in the early days of the faith when only a few, and those the best of men, were known by the name of monks, who as they received that mode of life from the evangelist Mark of blessed memory, the first to preside over the church of Alexandria as bishop, not only preserved those grand characteristics for which, we read, in the Acts of the Apostles, the church and the multitude of believers in primitive times was famous ("The multitude of believers had one heart and soul. Nor did any of them say that any of the things which he possessed was his own . ."), but they added to these characteristics others still more sublime."[53]

In the *Conferences*, he gives another description:

"And so the system of coenobites took its rise in the days of the preaching of the apostles. For such was all that multitude of believers in Jerusalem, which is thus described in the Acts of the Apostles: 'But the multitude of believers was one in heart and soul . . .' The whole Church, I say, was then such as those few who can be found with difficulty in coenobia."[54]

Colombas summarized this early view by saying:

> "The primitive Christian community of Jerusalem, as depicted in the Acts of the Apostles, was the ideal model which coenobites endeavored to reproduce. Moreover, they eventually came to see themselves as the successors of those fervent Christians who wished to follow the gospel teaching completely. There was a common theory that these first Christians were coenobitic monks."[55]

According to many ascetic teachers then, the reason for the formation of these "renewal communities" was an attempt to recover an integral part of Christian life—community (koinonia). In fact, the recovery of community life was an important concern in the ascetic movement. Pachomius saw community life, not ascetic life, as the most uniquely new feature of his foundations; and community remained a major concern for the Tabennesiot monks. Basil considered communal living definitely more Christian than eremetical living, and the entire movement in his diocese and surrounding regions of Asia Minor was apparently concerned largely with the restoration of community life. Augustine shared those concerns, as did many other leaders. The early ascetic movement, like some other renewal movements since and like the charismatic renewal today, contained a very important strand (ultimately the dominant strand) of concern for the restoration of communal life to Christianity. As in most other movements, other features of the renewal have overshadowed the communal element in people's attention, but it was, nonetheless, an important aspect of the ascetic movement.

The men mentioned above as examples of the ascetics' concern for community all lived in or founded coenobia, communities in which people's lives were in common. Coenobia were not, however, the only form of ascetic community. Ascetics grouped together in a variety of ways outside the normal structure of society, sometimes forming villages, sometimes forming districts on the edge of cities, sometimes forming just as a group of disciples around a spiritual father. In many of these groupings, community life was not a center of focus or concern; nevertheless, a form of community still came about. There was a natural human reason for that. When a person comes across something that is very important to him and that affects his whole life, as the new Christian life of the ascetic movement did, he naturally wants to share it with others and to live with those who have made that new ideal or experience the basis of their daily living. Community based on a shared ideal is a natural outgrowth of every movement of renewal. Those communities would not have to form separately from the lives of other Christians if everyone were to adopt the renewal form of Christian living. When everyone does not, however, it is natural for those in the renewal movement to want to group themselves together separately from the others.[56] Among the ascetics this desire was even stronger because their daily way of life was so different from the daily lives of most Christians.

It is a mistake to describe this formation of separate communities as "sectarian." It may be sectarian in a very broad sense of the term: the ascetics and ordinary Christians are divided in daily life. But in the most significant sense of the term it is not sectarian at all: the ascetics made no attempt to separate from the body of the Church and organize their own church. In fact, the formation of separate communities was anti-sectarian. Because the early ascetics had a different life and approach to Christianity, they were a potential source of disruption and conflict within a Christian grouping: a renewal group living within a group that has not accepted the renewal almost invariably causes tension and conflict. A common and effective way to deal with that difficulty is to separate the two groups so that those who want to live a "renewed life" can do so without forcing their approach on others. The history of religious orders demonstrates the effectiveness of this solution. The Observant, Reformed, and Capuchin Franciscans; the Discalced Carmelites; and the Trappists are all reformed branches which divided from religious orders. Even today religious orders and congregations are recognizing such division as a conceivable means of dealing with the tensions in their communities following the *aggiornamento* of the Vatican Council. "Renewal communities" are not necessarily sectarian. They are simply a way of avoiding a fundamental division by allowing different groups of people enough freedom to live their Christianity in some significantly different ways.

There was another reason for the formation of ascetic renewal communities. The fourth and fifth centuries were a time of tremendous change in the Christian Church. Two very significant things were happening: the relationship of the Church with society was changing so that a Christian society was emerging, and the number of Christians was growing rapidly because of Christianity's new status within the Roman Empire. The result was a massive social change within the Church. No longer were the Christians in each city relatively small groups with a tightly knit social structure of their own and a high degree of discipline and common identification. They were merging into society as a whole and losing their status as a separate environment. True, this change had occurred more extensively at the beginning of the fifth century than at the beginning of the fourth, but there are indications that the change had begun even before the conversion of Constantine.[57] The Christian world was definitely experiencing significant social change at the time of the ascetic movement's beginnings.

The result of the change the Church was undergoing was a rapid evolution in its structure. The Christians of the time were not as conscious of the structural change as they would be today. The fourth century did not think in the same historical and sociological terms as the twentieth. But the change was occurring. This was, for instance, the period of the formation of the parish system. It is difficult to trace the growth of parishes, but they apparently arose during this time as an answer to the growth in the number of Christians. As parishes developed, the Christians in each city were less unified as a body, and the bishop became less and less a direct pastor.[58] Another change was the gradual disappearance of the system of public penance. At the beginning of our period (305 A.D.) it was still used, but by the end (451) it was much less common. With the end of the public penance, the discipline of the Christian people changed as well.[59]

The diaconate was also gradually disappearing as an independent pastoral position. Deacons evolved into purely liturgical functionaries, while the functions they had once performed under the bishops were taken care of in other ways, ways which were increasingly institutional. Orphanages, poorhouses, and hospitals became more common, and the services once provided by the whole Christian people under the direction of the deacon were increasingly provided by Christian institutions.[60] All these changes developed gradually during the course of our period, but they point to an even more significant underlying change. Christians were less and less a cohesive environment, disciplined and able to perform its own social functions. They became more and more society itself. The Roman Empire became Christendom. And as the Church itself was experienced less as a body of people within society, it was experienced more as an institution or set of institutions providing religious services for society as a whole.

Before the ascetic movement began, ascetics lived their lives in and among other Christians. With the social structure of the Church before 300 A.D., Christian life was too tightly knit for them to form communities of their own without actually being divisive. But as the Church changed, ascetic communities became more possible. The loosening structure of Christian life made separate communities feasible.

There is some evidence, in fact, that many of the early ascetics believed their new communities were providing a better pastoral system for the Church. To be sure, the term "pastoral system" would not have appeared in the fourth century, but there was awareness of the need for changes in the church structure as evidenced by the frequency of councils and the embodiment of structural reform in new canons and there was evident dissatisfaction with church life and a desire for thoroughgoing reform. The Pachomian monasteries, according to Veuilleux,[61] were developed as a way to provide the Church with a better pastoral approach. They performed all the functions of church life, including evangelism and initiation. Basil, also, according to Gribomont,[62] understood the religious communities associated with him as the means to a pastoral renewal among the Christian people. The same goal may have been instinctively pursued by others as they grappled with the problems of pastoring a Christian people who were rapidly moving into a new Church age.

Communal Structures in the Ascetic Movement

The ascetics employed a variety of communal structures in forming their communities. Without understanding those structures, we cannot understand the way elders functioned within the ascetic movement or the meaning of the relationships between ascetic groups and the local bishops and churches. Relationships of leadership can rarely be adequately understood apart from the dynamics of the group in which those relationships function.

Many of the patterns ascetic life took could not actually be called communities, but would more properly be called settlements of ascetics. Ascetics gathered in many places without formal organization, much as they had before the ascetic movement began, except that their numbers grew much greater as the fourth century progressed. The *Historia Monachorum* has a description of Oxyrhynchus, a completely Christian city in Upper Egypt noted for the size of its monastic population. There is no trace of communal organization for the monks as a whole: they settled in the city in a variety of ways:

> "And we came also to Oxyrhyncus, a great city in the Thebaid, but we are not able to relate all the wonderful things which we saw therein; for the city is so full of habitations of the brethren that the walls are well nigh thrust out with them, so many are the brethren! And there are so many other monasteries[63] round about the walls, on the outside, that one

would think they were another city, and the sanctuaries of the city and the temples[64] which are therein, and all the spaces about them are filled with the monks. And besides these there were thirteen churches in which the people assembled, for the city was very large. There was a place set aside for the monks to pray in each of the monasteries, and one might think that the monks were not very much fewer in numbers than the ordinary inhabitants of the city, for they were so numerous that they even filled the buildings in the towers by the side of the city gates. Now the people said that the monks who lived inside were five thousand in number, and that five thousand brethren lived outside the city."[65]

The literature of the ascetic movement contains descriptions of many monastic settlements, the structure of whose common life is difficult to detect (if, indeed, it existed in a formal sense at all).

One particularly common form of ascetic settlement was the grouping of disciples around a spiritual master. The fame of some ascetics brought numerous disciples to live near them. As a result, temporary settlements, sometimes very large ones, grew up around great masters. Anthony was one of the first to gather disciples, and there was a large settlement at Pispir under his direction. Hilarion did the same; in fact, many men did. Many such settlements were isolated, but others such as those at Nitria and the Cells existed within larger settlements. Their only social structure was the individual's relationship to the spiritual father. When the master died, the settlement often ceased to exist.

There are three patterns of living which could more properly be described as communal, and these will provide the primary examples for discussing renewal communities. The first could be called the village structure. Many groups of ascetics formed into Christian villages, with a pattern of social organization similar to the villages nearby. From the Christian point of view, their structure was that of a local church. Often such villages would be found in the desert or some other place not normally inhabited. The chief example was Nitria, which was built southeast of Alexandria, not too far from the see-city of Hermopolis Parva (Damanhur), on a previously uninhabited hill bordering the desert. A famous description of Nitria in Palladius' *Lausiac History* gives a vivid picture of its village life:

> "On the mountain live close to five thousand men following different ways of life, each as he can or will. Thus some live alone, others in pairs, and some in groups. There are seven bakeries on this mountain serving these men as well as the hermits in the great desert, six hundred in all . . .

> "On this mountain of Nitria there is a great church in which stand three date palms, each with a whip hanging on it. Now one is for backsliding monks, another for any robbers that attack, the third for any robbers that happen by. All transgressors who are sentenced to a lashing are made fast to a date palm, and are freed when they have received the requisite number of lashes on the back.

> "The guesthouse is close to the church. Here the arriving guest is received until such time as he leaves voluntarily. He stays here all the time, even if for a period of two or three years. They allow a guest to remain at leisure for one week; from then on he must help in the garden, bakery, or kitchen. Should he be a noteworthy person, they give him a book, not allowing him to converse with anyone before the sixth hour. On this mountain there are doctors living and also pastry cooks. They use wine, too, and wine is sold.

> "All these work with their hands at making linen, so that none of them is in want. And indeed, along about the ninth hour, one can stand and hear the divine psalmody issuing forth from each cell and imagine one is high above paradise. They occupy the church on Saturdays and Sundays only.

Eight priests have charge of the church; while the senior priest lives, none of the others celebrates or gives the sermon, but they simply sit quietly by him."[66]

Not too far from Nitria was the Cells, where a smaller number of men lived an eremetic life, only gathering together for the liturgy on weekends. The Cells, too, had a presbyter at its head with other elders sharing some charge of the brothers.[67] Farther away, across the desert, was the valley of Scete in which there were four "congregations" organized along the lines of the Cells.[68] Nitria, the Cells, and Scete are mentioned here as the most famous of the monastic villages; however, the structure was apparently not uncommon elsewhere. Egeria, in her *Diary of a Pilgrimage*, described similar settlements in widely scattered parts of the Near East: on the peninsula of Sinai, at Carrhae in Mesopotamia, around the shrine of St. Thecla in Asia Minor.[69]

The second communal pattern of living is commonly termed the coenobium and is the pattern followed in most modern monasteries. Coenobia could be small or large, isolated by themselves or located in the middle of cities. In a coenobium, everything is done communally: coenobites not only hold their lives and resources in common, but they also administer them in common. There is a common rule of life, a common schedule, a common dwelling place, a common organization for work and for distribution of food and clothing. Nothing in anyone's life is outside the common life of the coenobium, and everything is under the direction of the head of the coenobium, the person we would call the abbot.

Pachomius is sometimes described as the father of the coenobium.[70] His monks considered him the originator of coenobitic life, and Tabenna the first coenobium. Certainly from Pachomius on, coenobia became more and more common. Basil's monasteries and those that follow his rule are coenobia as are those following the rule of Benedict. By the fifth century, most Egyptian cities as well as many rural districts had coenobia.

One variation of the coenobitic pattern bears some similarity to the village structure—the lavra. It was a common structure in Palestine where Euthymius and Sabas were perhaps the most famous founders, and it existed in other parts of the world as well. In terms of its pattern of life, the lavra is most like a village of hermits: the monks lived in separate cells in the neighborhood of a church and bakery, assembling on weekends for the liturgy, but spending most of their time as solitaries. Yet, in other ways, the lavra is like a coenobium:[71] it is organized in a similar way with an "abbot" and something like a rule. Moreover, lavras were often built in connection with a coenobium. Euthymius started a coenobium before starting a lavra;[72] Sabas' lavra operated in connection with Theodosius the Cenobiarch's coenobium.[73] Those who wanted to become ascetics would go first to the coenobium: it was their training ground. If, after a number of years, they seemed ready for a more solitary life, they would move to the lavra.

The Pachomian monasteries should be described here more fully, because, while clearly coenobia, they were unique among monasteries in the fourth century. They were unique first of all in their organization. Each coenobium had a highly developed structure of smaller houses within the larger coenobium and a system of heads and subordinate heads. In addition, all the coenobia were subordinate to the head of the Pachomian system, much as in a modern order. Finally, each coenobium was like both a self-sufficient village and a local church. Geographically, it was a village, and looked much like any other Coptic village; at the same time, it carried out all the functions of a church. Many ascetics first came to Tabennesiot monasteries as pagans. In the monastery they were instructed as Christians and then baptized at the annual Easter celebration for which all the monasteries were gathered. The Eucharist was celebrated within the monasteries after the earliest peried, and a penitential system was administered. As was mentioned above, the Tabennesiot monasteries were apparently conceived as a better pastoral system than the normal Egyptian church system of the time. They also bore many marks of an attempt to form a utopian society.

The third pattern of communal living could be called a coenobitical household. This term refers to a small grouping of ascetics living together in the pattern of a coenobium, but forming only a household grouping within a larger, non-ascetic community. They are not separated from the life of a normal Christian church, as the members of a coenobium are. Yet they have a common life that follows as many elements of the coenobitic life as possible. Probably the most famous example of this pattern is Augustine's episcopal household in Hippo, a household of clerics leading a common life yet serving in the church at Hippo.[74] It is likely that many monasteries under Basil's care as bishop were small households of ascetics who lived in a village or city and served the local Christians.[75] Ambrose refers to Eusebius of Vercelli as the first to bring the life of the monks into the city and to unite the rules of clerics and monks.[76] Sozomen tells us that the monk Melos, who became bishop of Rhinocorura in southern Palestine, established a household like this with his clergy. "The clergy of this church dwell in one house, sit at the same table, and have everything in common."[77] Paulinus of Nola lived a similar life with his clergy.[78] Augustine, in *De moribus ecclesiae catholicae* refers to houses in Milan and Rome that were made up of laymen living a common life together.[79]

As we think about the ascetic movement as a renewal movement in the early Church, and as we think about the relationships of renewal communities to the local church, we must realize that we are dealing with a popular movement that did not have one pattern of organization handed on from group to group. The early ascetic movement took many different forms. Only as some of the rules, like Basil's and Benedict's, gained in prestige did any measure of uniformity develop. When the bishops dealt with the early ascetic movement, they were dealing with a number of very different situations.

III
Unordained Elders in
Patristic Tradition

We have considered fourth century asceticism as a movement of renewal, and have examined the growth of renewal communities (monasteries) within that movement. With that perspective on the early ascetic movement, it is possible to draw lessons from the movement's history for the integration of renewal communities into the life of the Church as a whole. The first principle that emerges is that the unordained elder is an important figure within the tradition of the Church, not an abuse. Even a cursory investigation of the early ascetic movement shows that unordained elders existed, that they exercised all the pastoral functions of ordained elders, except for certain sacramental functions, and that they were supported by the authorities of the Church in their pastoral work. Some of the greatest saints and fathers of the Church served as unordained elders, either for their whole lives or for periods of their lives.

The question of unordained elders is not usually considered in connection with the early ascetic movement and it does not reappear in later movements that developed within the ascetic tradition (like the mendicant movement). That is largely because the majority of monks from the early Middle Ages on were ordained. Modern Catholics, in fact, often assume that all monks are priests. Yet, as recent discussions on this question have pointed out,[80] the ordination of monks is a relatively recent phenomenon. At first, there were no ordained ascetics (except for an occasional cleric who adopted the ascetic life), then only a few were ordained for the

36

service of the ascetic communities. It was not until a much later period than the one under consideration that ordination of ascetics became normative.

To understand the full significance of the existence of unordained elders, it is necessary to consider a fact sometimes obscured by terminology. The official leaders of the Roman Catholic Church, the Orthodox and other Eastern churches, and (often) the churches of the Anglican communion are most commonly referred to in English as "priests." Their official Greek title is "presbyteros" (Anglicized: "presbyter"), the Greek term for "elder." *Presbyteros* is the word used in the New Testament to designate the elders of the Christian communities. Elders, in other words, are the official heads of the Christian people (usually under the presidency of the bishop) who perform the pastoral functions of the church in virtue of their office. And the "priests" of the Catholic Church are "the elders" of the Catholic Church.

When we talk about unordained elders, then, we are speaking of people who perform the role of the elders of the church, but who are not ordained. We are discussing the exercise of a pastoral ministry by someone who has not been ordained presbyter. On the face of it, such a thing seems at least irregular. Many nowadays consider the very idea dangerous, and consider the people who speak of it somewhat un-Catholic (because they seem to be disrespecting the sacrament of orders). Yet history shows that the unordained elder is an old Catholic tradition, that the position was allowed and even encouraged by bishops in the Patristic age for very good pastoral reasons, and that the unordained elder arose precisely in the context of a renewal movement as a means of bringing order into that movement. Rather than being un-Catholic, the idea of the unordained elder is an excellent example of that very flexibility which has always characterized Catholic tradition.[81]

The Founders as Unordained Elders

Two fairly distinct types of unordained elders operated within the structures of the early ascetic movement: <u>founding</u> elders and "<u>supplementary</u> elders." The earliest leaders of the movement best represent the first type. These were the men most responsible for the growth of the ascetic movement. They embraced the ascetic life and then lived it in a very successful, impressive way. Many reached the point of having charismatic powers: inspired knowledge, prophecy, healing, miracle-working, the ability to discern and cast out demons.[82] Attracted by their example, disciples gathered around these great ascetics, eager to live the same life. The ascetics found themselves, at times almost unwillingly, the spiritual leaders of large numbers of Christians.

Leadership in the early stages of any movement usually arises spontaneously. The sociologist Weber popularized the term "charismatic" to describe leadership based on the special gifts or special powers of an individual, and such "charismatic leadership" is precisely the kind that makes movements possible. Because a movement involves new social forms, charismatic leadership is often the only effective leadership possible in its early stages. Later, as movements mature and social patterns emerge, leadership patterns can develop that will allow positions of leadership to emerge on other bases. But spontaneous leadership appears first. Although Weber's term is sociological and not theological (the "charisma" he refers to is simply a natural gift and does not necessarily involve a work of the Holy Spirit), there is a Christian parallel to the sociological concept. The New Testament teaches that God gives men the gifts to be Christian leaders: the ability to be a pastor or teacher or apostle depends on a gift of God. If that is true, someone can have an authentic gift of spiritual leadership without having yet been given an official position of leadership within the Christian people. Modern Catholic theologians are recognizing and stressing this truth. In short, the kind of "charismatic" leadership that is exercised in the early stages of a renewal movement can be genuinely a gift of the Holy Spirit. The Christians in the Patristic period recognized that fact, as is indicated by the fact that so many of these charismatic leaders, ordained or not, were venerated as saints.[83]

Anthony the Great most clearly typifies the first leaders of the ascetic movement who functioned as elders. He taught and ruled the men gathered around him as a Christian pastor. All evidence indicates that he was not ordained. Indeed, he made a point of honoring the clergy over himself.[84] Pachomius, also, the man who established an "improved pastoral system" and became the effective Christian pastor of thousands, was not only unordained, but actually resisted ordination out of humility.[85] Ammon of Nitria, Hilarion, Julian Saba, Abraham Qidunaia, Simon Estonia, and Benedict were among the more outstanding men who were never ordained yet functioned as elders. Macarius of Egypt, Macarius of Alexandria, Basil of Caesarea, Jerome, Augustine, Sabas, and Gregory the Great all functioned for some time as unordained elders before being ordained to serve as either ordained elders in their ascetic communities or as ordained elders for a local church.

While some unordained elders presided over groups composed essentially of personal disciples, groups lasting only as long as the master, others established communities, both villages and coenobia, which outlived their founders. Some of these groups had a succession of unordained elders as heads. Both the early Benedictine and the early Basilian communities seem to have been usually headed by unordained elders (although their modern descendants are usually headed by abbots who have previously been ordained presbyters).

The unordained elders who were founders or early leaders of monastic groups exercised a wide range of pastoral functions. In fact, since presbyters (ordained elders) in the first centuries did not usually celebrate the Eucharist or reconcile penitents canonically, it would even be correct to say that the unordained ascetic elders exercised all the *normal* pastoral functions of presbyters in the early Church. First of all, they taught, and they taught with authority. Many men listed above were famous as teachers. All the unordained elders regularly gathered those under them to instruct them in Christian living and sometimes Christian doctrine.[86] They also directed their monks as a shepherd would, guiding their lives in an authoritative way. In fact, they exercised a firmer and more constant pastoral authority in the lives of those men than did the bishops or clergy of the day.[87] Finally, they disciplined their monks, just as a bishop disciplined his people through penance.

To understand the significance of monastic penitential discipline, it is necessary to consider the difference between the penitential practice of the early Church and penitential practice today. Today in the Catholic and Orthodox Churches, penance is usually private, except in cases of grave public scandal. The sinner is his own accuser and goes to the priest (ordained presbyter) privately. The priest instructs him about the nature of the sin if necessary, assigns him "a penance," and then gives him absolution. Penance is experienced as spiritual counseling (authoritative counseling, to be sure), not as a judicial procedure. Penance in the early Church, however, was a disciplinary, judicial process. If the sinner did not take the initiative, one of the elders or the bishop would. The sinner was cut off from communion and, if he remained impenitent, from the whole life of the Church. If he repented, he would remain out of communion for a time but was given a special place within the Christian community that allowed a limited participation in its life. During that time, he was expected to perform such penitential practices as fasting and almsgiving. When the bishop was satisfied that the penitent had so changed that his life would continue to be different, he was reconciled. The process was clearly disciplinary and judicial as well as curative.

The same process of public penance was practiced in those monastic communities we know most about. In the Pachomian monasteries, the penitential practice involved exclusion from the common life. This included exclusion from communion and a period of penance as well as reconciliation by the superior (praepositus) of the monastery.[88] A similar procedure was followed in Basilian communities. The superior of a Basilian brotherhood, who was normally not ordained, was responsible for the discipline of the brothers, and could both exclude and reconcile them as necessary, although in Basil's rule no stipulations are made for the position of a penitent in semi-exclusion.[89] Finally, the rule of St.

Benedict contains a description of a penitential procedure which corresponds to the practice of public penance in the early Church. For impenitents, it involved exclusion; for those repenting of serious sin, it called for remedial semi-exclusion, including penitential practices (exclusion from communion) and reconciliation.[90] Most rules we still have from ascetic communities show this same procedure. There was practiced, in addition, a penitential counsel in which a brother opened his life to a superior or elder, confessing sin in order to receive help in overcoming it, but this penitential counseling did not replace the communal public penance.

To say that the ascetic communities used the same penitential practice as the early Church is not to say that unordained elders administered what a modern Catholic would refer to as the sacrament of penance. It is true that ascetic communities, including those headed by unordained superiors, practiced a disciplinary, judicial penitential procedure identical in its main outlines to the penitential practice of the early Church. Yet at the same time, there is no clear recorded instance of an ascetic who, having fallen into a sin subject to canonical penances, was then reconciled by an unordained elder without the intervention of a bishop or ordained presbyter in the process. Without such evidence, no claim that unordained elders administered the sacrament of penance can be substantiated. The heads of the ascetic communities, in other words, exercised within their communities the normal disciplinary functions that ordained elders exercised in the Church at large. They excluded people for disorder and sin, imposed penances, and reconciled penitents to the ascetic community when the problem had been taken care of. They exercised a pastoral function in the area of penance, but they did not exercise a function Catholics would recognize as administering the sacrament of penance.[91]

The unordained elders and their communities were by no means on the edge of the Christian people or under suspicion by the ordained clergy.[92] By that I do not mean to imply that there were never any difficulties. But on the whole, the founders of the ascetic movement were supported by the bishops of the time. In many ways, the growth of the ascetic movement in Egypt was due to the support that Athanasius gave it. Besides generally encouraging the movement, he was a close friend and supporter of Anthony. His biography of Anthony became one of the most influential books on behalf of the movement. He also supported Pachomius and his monks warmly, as did many bishops of Egypt. One bishop, in fact, sent someone to Pachomius to do penance, thus entrusting an unordained elder with a pastoral responsibility precisely in the area of the official penitential discipline.[93] Later, Gregory the Great promoted Benedict and his approach to ascetic life much as Athanasius had promoted Anthony, even becoming Benedict's principal biographer as Athanasius had been Anthony's. Some scholars attribute the widespread influence the rule of Benedict has had in the West to Gregory's support. There was, in short, a great deal of support from ordained leaders of the Church, including the greatest bishops of the age, for the work of the unordained leaders of the ascetic movement.

Supplementary Elders

Another kind of unordained elder common in the ascetic movement was the elder who was not necessarily the head or founder of an ascetic community, but who contributed to the pastoral leadership as part of a college of elders. Most ascetic communities had a group of elders who took a pastoral concern for the brothers as a whole. This did not ordinarily happen in the groupings composed mainly of disciples gathered around a master, but wherever ascetics formed some community structure, one could usually find a group of elders.

The existence of a body of unordained elders is most easily seen in the communities following the village pattern. Because Nitria, Cells, and Scete are the best documented examples of the village system, a clear record remains of their leadership structures. In all three locations, unordained elders functioned under an ordained presbyter. At Cells there seems to have been one presbyter with supporting unordained elders[94]; at Scete each congregation had an ordained presbyter with a group of unordained elders[95]; at Nitria a group of presbyters served under a head presbyter[96], but there is some evidence that a group of unordained elders existed as well.

The functioning of a group of unordained elders under a presbyter is illustrated most clearly in Cassian's picture of the congregation of Paphnutius at Scete.[97] While Paphnutius was clearly the head of the congregation, functioning much like a bishop,[98] the elders as a whole took a pastoral responsibility for the brothers. They met together as a group to discuss questions. They decided together on the teaching that was given.[99] They taught the other brothers, doing a lot of what we might call pastoral counseling, although their counseling was authoritative (directive), that is, they expected obedience.[100]

Cassian's picture of Scete is supplemented by the *Apophthegmata Patrum*. There we not only see the elders teaching, but also administering a penitential discipline.[101] They corrected sinners, decided on how to handle difficult cases, excluded those who were impenitent, and apparently reconciled the penitent.[102] The elders governed their communities, taking concern for the distribution of money, the care of the needy, relations with groups outside of the community, and even choosing candidates for ordination.[103]

There were also groups of unordained elders in the coenobia. They functioned somewhat differently than the elders in ascetic villages. Since the members of a coenobium did everything together, the superior was responsible for the whole life of the community including providing food, clothing, and shelter as well as giving pastoral direction. He functioned somewhat like the head of a tribe or a father of a family, concerned not only with the spiritual welfare of the people but also with their economic life. As a result, the elders in a coenobium could not function by simply overseeing the general life of the community and correcting what was wrong as the village elders did. They had to direct every aspect of the community's life and work.

To meet the special conditions in the coenobium, a number of leadership systems developed. Pachomius[104] used a clear system of subgroupings with subordinate heads. Each monastery was broken down into houses of thirty or forty monks under a house superior. Those superiors were in turn subject to the superior of the monastery (the father of the monastery). The house superiors as well as the father taught, directed, and disciplined the monks, and they were apparently called elders. The system established in Basil's rules[105] seems closer to that of an ascetic village. There were two groups among the brothers, those who were entrusted with leadership and those who obeyed.[106] Those entrusted with leadership are usually referred to as superiors, sometimes even as presbyters although it seems clear that they were not ordained. This group existed alongside the main superior and assisted him in the care of the brotherhood. Benedict[107] used a somewhat different system. All the brothers were ranked according to the date they entered the community, so that each person had both elders and juniors. He was directed to obey his elders. In addition, the oldest of the elders apparently functioned at times as a special group. Moreover, in larger communities "deans" were appointed to take responsibility for sub-groupings. In summary, there were unordained elders in coenobia as well as in ascetic villages, but the way they functioned varied.

The pastoral structure that emerges as we study the renewal communities of ascetics was modelled on the structure of the Church. Instead of a bishop, there was the superior of the community, who in many cases was ordained. Working along with the superior, sharing the pastoral care but under his direction, are a body of elders. Their actual pastoral practices varied, just as they varied among the local churches, but the pattern was the same. The ascetic communities apparently adopted the pattern of the church around them as they structured their pastoral leadership.

Parallelism

Despite the effort many scholars have made to create the impression that the ascetic movement was anti-ecclesiastical or anti-clerical, there is no instance in which the ascetic movement deva-lued the ordained clergy or refused to be subordinate to any bishop (until the rise of Messalianism toward the end of the fourth centu-ry in Syria and Asia Minor). Respect and submission was given to the bishop and clergy. Respect was also shown for ordination and for the difference it made in the authority of the person or-dained.[108]

One way in which the difference between ordained and unor-dained elders was kept clear was the matter of terminology. Al-most universally, different terms were used for the ordained elders and the unordained elders. The Greek word for the ordained elder was always *presbyteros*. He was also at times referred to as the priest *(hiereus)*.[109] The word most commonly used in ascetic litera-ture for the unordained elder was *geron*, which is sometimes trans-lated "old man."[110] Like *elder*, both *presbyteros* and *geron* sim-ply mean "an older person." But in many societies around the world, the natural leaders of a communal grouping are called the elders; that is, "elder" refers not just to those who are oldest, but to those among the older members of a community who have been chosen to govern. The Jewish people had their elders for each village and for the nation as a whole. That pattern was followed for each body of Jews in the diaspora as well. The Egyptian vil-lages had their elders, as did the Syrian. In short, the term "elder" is naturally used not just of those of greater age, but also of those among the older men who are the rulers of a people. The early Christians followed this ancient pattern when they used a Greek word meaning older man to describe their rulers, the presbyters. When the ascetic movement came along, it made use of a different Greek word meaning old man to describe those of its rulers who were not ordained. Using a different word with the same meaning allowed the ascetics to designate a position of identical function while preserving a clarity about the difference in authority.

That pattern was also followed in Latin. Latin-speaking Christians borrowed the Greek word for elder to describe their ordained leaders, the *presbyteri*,[111] and also at times referred to them as "priests" *(sacerdotes)*. When the Western ascetic movement came along, the same thing happened in Latin that happened in Greek. The word *presbyter* was reserved for those who were ordained elders and other words were pressed into service to describe unordained elders. Most common was *seniores* (literally "elder," the normal Latin term for "elder") and *senes* (literally "old men"). Another commonly used word was *maiores* meaning literally "greater ones," which ordinarily designated the greater in age (the older son could be described as *maior*).

Some other terms used in ascetic literature to designate unordained elders are worth observing simply for clarity's sake. A common designation in both Greek and Latin was "father"; unordained elders were often referred to as "fathers" either in the vernacular or by using the Semitic "abba." Another frequently used word was *superior* (*proestos* in Greek, *praepositus* in Latin). The head of the Basilian brotherhoods was called the superior as were the subordinate heads in Pachomian monasteries and the heads in Augustine's monasteries.

Within the ascetic movement, then, a clear distinction was maintained between the unordained elders and the ordained elders. The word *presbyteros* or *presbyter* was reserved for the ordained elder, and it was clear to all that he had an authority the unordained elder did not. Nonetheless, the unordained elders were called by terms parallel to those used for the ordained elders, and performed parallel functions. The two positions were, in short, parallel, except that the ordained elders were the official heads and pastors of the Christian community and hence could perform certain official (sacramental) functions that the unordained elders could not. The unordained elders were only the heads and pastors of members of renewal communities clearly subordinate to the Church as a whole.

Another example of parallelism should be pointed out. The early ascetics consistently applied those scriptural texts originally directed to the local church and to the ordained clergy (or apostles) to their own communities and unordained elders or superiors.[112] The Tabennesiots, for instance, applied most of the scriptural terms for the Church to their community.[113] Pachomius himself used the passage "whatever you bind on earth shall be bound in heaven and whatever you loose on earth shall be loosed in heaven" to establish his authority in the area of penance.[114] Basil applied the concept of the body of Christ found in 1 Corinthians 12 to his brotherhoods of ascetics, and the instructions on excommunication from 1 Corinthians 5 to exclusion as practiced in his brotherhoods. He also applied a number of the passages with which Paul described his own apostolic service to the service of the superior of his brotherhoods.[115] Benedict used "He who hears you hears me" (Luke 10:16) to enjoin obedience to the abbot and also used 1 Corinthians 5 to explain exclusion from the monastery.[116] Numerous other examples are easily found, but the point is simple. Respected saints and teachers, fathers of the Church, applied texts that refer to the Church to their ascetic communities and used texts that justify the authority of ordained elders to establish the authority of unordained elders. They apparently felt no need to justify such interpretation and did not question whether the passages actually should be applied to unordained leaders.

We are confronted here with a phenomenon common to renewal movements. As a movement for renewal develops, and renewal communities spring up, the question of structure and order arises. The pattern Christians naturally adopt is the "Christian pattern"—the structural patterns taught in the Scriptures and followed in the wider Christian community. Renewal communities always tend to pattern themselves on the New Testament church. They have elders and pastoral authority and penitential discipline. They see themselves as an authentic expression of the Church's life and conduct themselves accordingly.[117]

At the same time, within the Catholic tradition, such communities do not claim to be on the level of the Church as a whole. They are communities within the Church, subject to the bishop. The early ascetic movement was well-integrated within the life of the Church of the time and was not rebellious. It was, to be sure, a parallel structure, but a parallel structure that was supported and encouraged by the bishops.

The position of unordained elder, then, is not an abuse. It is rather a Patristic tradition, a tradition that has been of real service within the Church. It is, moreover, a very natural development. Unordained elders did not appear within the ascetic movement in response to any theory. No one taught that unordained elders were needed, nor did anyone, either the bishops or those involved in the ascetic movement, create them as a matter of strategy. Rather they emerged naturally within a particular situation, in a time when the Church was experiencing social change and a new movement was developing. Since the old leadership patterns of church life were not adequate to the new situation, new leadership patterns emerged naturally ("charismatically") that were essential for both the health of the new movement and its good order within the Church. It was the unordained elders who corrected abuses within the movement and maintained its good relationship with the Church as a whole. The bishops were not in a good position to do so because they were outside the movement.

The unordained elder, then, is an instrument of pastoral flexibility. The role is valuable precisely when leadership is needed in some new situation, but it is not clear how that leadership should be related to existing structures. In the beginning stages of any social development the leadership structures should remain informal and flexible, both because those in the new movement are not sure of the direction and shape they will eventually take and because those in more established positions of leadership are not sure how to relate to the new development. Unordained elders allow healthy innovation.

Unordained elders can also supplement existing leadership patterns. Early bishops normally did not want to ordain a large number of presbyters for ascetic communities, because, as will be considered further on, including that many ascetics in the diocesan college of presbyters would create an imbalance in the pastoral leadership of the Church. Unordained elders provided the ascetic communities the leadership they needed without making a major increase in the number of diocesan presbyters. In short, the "institution" of the unordained elder was very helpful to the patristic church in constructively integrating the ascetic movement into its total life.

IV
Ordination and
Renewal Communities

The previous section was mainly concerned with unordained elders as a genuine and valuable Catholic tradition. Concentrating only on the existence and role of unordained elders, however, leaves a onesided picture. While unordained elders did exist and ascetic communities did exist in which no one was ordained, normally an official link was expressed between the ascetic communities and the leadership structure of the larger Church by ordination. In fact, the history of the ascetic movement in the fourth and fifth centuries teaches the principle that the normal way to relate a renewal community to the Church as a whole is to ordain its leader(s) to the presbyterate of the diocese in which the community is situated.

Ordaining Ascetic Leaders

From a very early time in the history of the ascetic movement, the bishops who had ascetic groupings in their diocese were concerned that the leaders of those groupings, at least the leaders who had genuine pastoral responsibilities, be ordained presbyters. There were, of course, a fair number of men who had been ordained presbyters before joining an ascetic group, but bishops seem to have been concerned to see that the heads of the communities be ordained presbyters.[118] There were important exceptions. We have no evidence that Anthony was ever ordained presbyter, nor is there any recorded attempt by a bishop to ordain him. Pachomius once resisted an attempt by his bishop, Sapron, to ordain him.[119] At least during their early history, the Tabennesiot monks imitated him in avoiding ordination, making use of the services of a nearby presbyter for the Eucharist. But in general the heads of the ascetic communities either were ordained willingly or at least gave in to ordination.

In Nitria, Cells, and Scete, ordination was normal for the leaders of the communities.[120] Pambo, one of the more prominent Nitrian ascetics, was ordained fairly early, probably before 340 (i.e., within fifteen years of the first settlement at Nitria). The *Letter of Ammon* preserves a letter written by Theodore the Tabennesiot about 356 which is addressed "To the beloved brethren, the presbyters and deacons and monks in the mountain of Nitria." The *Letter of Ammon* also mentions four presbyters at Nitria—Pambo, Pior, Heraclides, and Hagius—and Palladius' description quoted above refers to a college of eight priests. Cells, an offshoot of Nitria, had its own presbyter—Macarius of Alexandria at one time held that position. Scete was first settled by Macarius of Egypt before he was ordained. He and the other brothers would walk forty miles across the desert to attend the liturgy celebrated by Pambo at Nitria. The *Apophthegmata* tells of a visit Macarius once paid to Anthony, asking advice on problems in Scete. He told the elders on his return that Anthony had singled out as the biggest problem Scete's lack of a Eucharist. Macarius himself was eventually ordained presbyter and by the time of Cassian's visit to Scete (ca. 393) there were four congregations each with a presbyter at the head. Cassian visited one under the leadership of the presbyter Paphnutius, successor to presbyter Isidore. Cassian relates Paphnutius' attempt to insure a worthy successor by having Daniel ordained; Daniel, however, died before Paphnutius.[121]

We have records of other village-type settlements similar to Nitria and Scete.[122] Dorotheus was the presbyter for the anchorites at Antinoe, apparently serving much as Paphnutius at Scete or Macarius at Cells. Romun performed the same service for the anchorites at Diolcos. Cronmius was presbyter for a fairly large group of ascetics in a structure probably more like a village than a coenobium.

The practice was also common in the coenobia. A general consensus seems to have emerged fairly early throughout the East that the heads of coenobia should be ordained. Sapron, as was mentioned above, tried to ordain Pachomius. The records show presbyters such as Hor, Appelles, Eulogius, and Dioscoros, governing communities of ascetics throughout Egypt that were likely coenobia.[123] In Jerusalem, Rufinus' community had its own presbyter, Innocent, and later Rufinus himself was ordained.[124] Jerome fought a constant battle to keep bishops away, but was finally ordained against his will. When he thereafter refused to officiate as presbyter for his Bethlehem community, Epiphanius, the bishop of Salamis and a former monk, ordained Jerome's brother Paulinian to the displeasure of both Jerome and his bishop, John of Jerusalem.[125] Egeria found ascetic communities presided over by presbyters in the Sinai and Palestine.[126] From Asia Minor we have records of Elpidius and Sisinnus, who were ordained presbyters to head coenobia.[127] By the fifth century it was apparently common practice to ordain men to the presbyterate if they were the heads of coenobia or lavras; indeed, the Council of Chalcedon lists monasteries along with city parish churches, village churches, and shrines of martyrs as normal positions for presbyters.[128] By the latter half of the century, resistance to ordination by someone like Sabas stands out, and even he was eventually forced to it by his bishop.[129]

The records of those ordained to be heads of monastic communities are not complete, to be sure. However, there was apparently not much controversy about whether the practice was right or not. It was taken as a matter of course, except by those monks who wanted to have nothing to do with ordination, usually for motives of humility. The literature does not make the matter of ordination a central focus, and often the title presbyter seems synonymous with abbot, that is, the head of the community.[130] Consequently it is sometimes unclear if someone was actually ordained specifically to be head of the coenobium or if he had been ordained before beginning to live the ascetic life.

There are, in addition, records of men who were ordained bishops because they were the heads of ascetic communities. Timothy, in Cappadocia, was a chorbishop (something like today's auxiliary bishop) and even after his death it seems to have been common for the head of his community to be a chorbishop.[131] Perhaps his community was the chief ascetic grouping in the diocese and the head was therefore appointed chorbishop to provide pastoral care for all the ascetics in the diocese (chorbishops were often given supervision of monks, especially those outside the see city). Sozomen mentions a number of ascetics who were ordained bishops because they were outstanding men, but not appointed to an existing see. Rather, they were allowed to continue in their communities:

> "Barses and Eulogius were both ordained bishops, but not of any city; for the title was merely an honorary one, conferred on them as a compensation for their excellent conduct; and they were ordained in their own monasteries. Lazarus, to whom we have already alluded, was ordained bishop in the same manner."[132]

What comes to mind in this context is the later Western institution of mitered abbots. There seems to have been a recurrent tendency to assimilate the position of head of a large coenobium to that of bishop.

To keep the picture clear, we should call to mind something which has already been mentioned—many coenobia had unordained heads, even after the early stages of the ascetic movement. Apparently, Basil's brotherhoods did not ordinarily have ordained heads, although some probably did, nor did the small ascetic communities under Augustine in North Africa. Somewhat after our period, we can see from the rule of St. Benedict and the *Dialogues* of Gregory the Great that the first communities following or influenced by the Benedictine rule did not always (or usually) have ordained presbyters as their abbots, nor did many other monasteries in Italy in the period. Apparently, the larger communities were more likely to have ordained presbyters as heads than the smaller. Basil's, Augustine's, and Benedict's communities were smaller than those in Egypt, Syria, and Palestine. Ordination of the head might also have been more likely for a community isolated in the country than for one located in the city near a bishop and adequate college of presbyters.

On the whole, the initiative for ordaining the heads of ascetic communities to the presbyterate seems to have come from the bishops. Indeed, we have already seen instances in which the ascetic leaders themselves actually resisted ordination. Yet the bishops were not alone in wanting the ordinations: the monks wanted them too.[133] Athanasius, attempting to persuade Dracontius to remain a bishop rather than return to the monastic life, counters some of Dracontius' monastic advisers by saying:

> "And why do they advise you not to take up the bishop's office, when they themselves wish to have presbyters? For if you are bad, let them not associate with you. But if they know that you are good, let them not envy the others. For if, as they say, teaching and government is an occasion of sin, let them not be taught themselves, nor have presbyters, lest they deteriorate, both they and those who teach them."[134]

Clearly, Athanasius was feeling a certain pressure from the monks to have presbyters appointed. Both bishops and monks felt it was an appropriate way to meet the sacramental and governmental needs of the ascetic communities.

The bishops not only appointed presbyters to head individual monastic communities, they also tended to appoint someone, usually a monk, to function under themselves as the head of the monks in the diocese.[135] Such individuals were sometimes titled archimandrite or exarch of all the monks. The institution apparently rose in the closing decades of the fourth century. In the *Historia Monachorum* (written about 393) we find Serapion responsible for all the ascetics of the diocese of Arsinoe:

> "And we also saw in the regions of Arsinoites a certain elder

whose name was Serapion; he was the father of all the monasteries, and head of numerous brotherhoods, which contained about ten thousand men."[136]

Shortly after the beginning of the fifth century, Euthymius was appointed head of all the monks of Melitene in Lesser Armenia, from which position he promptly fled to be a hermit in the Judean desert. By the Council of Chalcedon, the position of the archimandrite of all the monks in the diocese was common in many cities of the East, most notably in Constantinople where Eutyches himself held that position. Only in Syrian countries was the position missing. The archimandrite held a very powerful position. He was more than a simple Vicar for Religious, he was almost the bishop for religious, a pastoral head subordinate only to the bishop of the diocese. In one instance in 492, the patriarch Sallust in Jerusalem appointed two archimandrites, Sabas for the hermits (mainly living in lavras) and Theodosius the Cenobiarch for the coenobites, but in general there was only one head for all those following the ascetic life. In other words, by the middle of the fifth century, many bishops had established a special pastoral structure for those who were part of the ascetic movement, a pastoral structure that was under the direction of the bishop, but that was parallel to the normal pastoral structure of the diocese.

Bishops and Renewal Communities

The early bishops tended to want to ordain the heads of renewal communities to be presbyters in order to see that pastoral government and sacramental ministry were adequately cared for. From all that we can see in the literature, the approach was either obviously the right one or at least taken for granted. Moreover, as a pastoral strategy it fit in well with what was happening in the church of the period.

It has already been established that the third, the fourth, and the early fifth centuries were times of great pastoral change for the Christian Church in the Roman Empire. The increasing identification of the state with the Christian religion and the large influx of new converts resulted in a demand for looser structures that could accommodate more people. The bishops consequently made changes in their pastoral structures. Throughout the period sub-groupings were formed in the diocese with presbyters at their head.[137] The need was first felt in the country. At the beginning of the century, the institution of chorbishops, traveling auxiliary bishops who cared for the Christians in outlying villages, was common. Chorbishops were supplemented and eventually replaced by parishes with presbyters set over them. Something similar happened in the cities, where presbyters were set over pastoral districts. These head presbyters (we would call them "pastors" in English) functioned under the bishop but they had almost complete pastoral responsibility for the people in their charge. The one function clearly reserved to the bishop was the ordination of new presbyters. Other functions, often including penitential discipline,[138] were in the hands of the presbyters.

In this context, it is not so strange to see bishops ordaining the heads of the ascetic communities. The bishop was simply taking those who actually had the pastoral direction of large groups of people and joining them to the college of elders with which he governed the diocese. It was a very intelligent way to unite two systems of pastoral government—the system that served the ascetic communities and the diocesan system. At the same time, he was also establishing special parishes with their own presbyters, following the general approach he was taking with other villages and districts in his diocese. The ascetic "parishes" were even territorial parishes, since the ascetics tended to live together, separate from other Christians.

As was pointed out above in the discussion of "supplementary elders," there was a tendency, especially in the groupings described as village structures, to reproduce within the ascetic community the diocesan structure. A presbyter would be in charge, but serving with him would be a group of unordained elders. The presbyter functioned like the bishop of the community;[139] the unordained elders functioned like presbyters. Thus, the ascetic community operated according to the model of the diocese within the framework of the local diocese. We might naturally ask here why the bishop did not ordain the unordained elders as well as the chief presbyter. While nothing in the early literature answers this question (it never seems to have been raised), it is not difficult to propose some reasons. For one thing, the ascetic communities had many more elders than an equivalent sized grouping in the normal diocesan structure. They had more elders both because the intensity of their life together as Christians called for more pastoral care and direction and because in a body of men like the ascetics there were many more who were qualified to be elders. As a result, if the bishop were to ordain all the monastic elders as presbyters, the presbyterate of most dioceses would have been predominantly monks in ascetic communities. That would have given the ascetics an even heavier influence than they already had. A second reason for not ordaining all the monastic elders was probably the effect it would have had on the relationship between the presbyter of the ascetic community and the bishop. Had all the unordained ascetic elders been ordained, the head presbyter might easily have become another bishop with a large number of presbyters under him. There would no longer have been a natural method of subordination. As it was, the presbyter of the ascetic community was clearly subordinate to the bishop and the unordained elders were clearly subject to the presbyter. A final reason that should be noted is that there was no need to ordain them. The main function which the presbyter could perform that the other elders could not was to preside at the Eucharist. In an ascetic community there was only one celebration; so only one president was needed. At that time, presbyters were not ordained if they were not needed. The practice of ordaining monks as presbyters even when they were not needed was not introduced until much later, when the concept of a presbyter had already changed significantly.[140]

When bishops ordained the heads of the ascetic communities, they respected the autonomy of the community. To be sure, the bishop had authority over who would be ordained, but he did not simply ordain any competent man as presbyter of a particular community. Almost always, in fact, the man he ordained was either already the head of the community or had just been chosen the head. This tradition is still followed within the Church. Bishops do not choose the abbots of monasteries or the superiors of religious communities. They sometimes have the right to confirm the choice of the community, but each community is free to choose its own head. There is even canonical legislation from the period shortly after ours in which bishops are forbidden to appoint the heads of the ascetic communities under them. Nor do bishops have the right to ordain any members of the community they choose. If someone from the community is to be ordained presbyter, he is put forward by the head of the community, not by the bishop. As it says in the rule of St. Benedict, "If an abbot desires to have a priest or a deacon ordained for his monastery, let him choose one of his monks who is worthy to exercise the priestly office."[141]

There is a reason why the early bishops respected the autonomy of the local community in the choice of those who were to be ordained as its heads. Not to respect the autonomy of a community in the choice of its leaders is to destroy the community or to absorb it into another. Within every community, there is a natural leadership structure. When that structure is not followed in the appointment of leaders, the community does not function as well. And it is those within the community who are most conscious of that leadership structure, and who should therefore choose the head.[142] Moreover, it is rare that someone who is not a member of a community could come to that community as its head and be able to unite it as a community.

In the Catholic Church today, the bishopric and the presbyterate have been institutionalized. We deal with something more like a service institution than a communal structure.[143] Consequently, an ordained leader can be moved from one position to another without seriously impairing his ability to function. The Church of the fourth and fifth centuries was more communally structured, and the bishops were conscious of the need to conform leadership structures to communal dynamics. This was true not only in choosing heads for ascetic communities, but also in choosing heads of the Church itself. Bishops and presbyters were chosen out of the people they would serve. They would stay among those people for the rest of their lives and not be transferred to a "better" see. Many canons forbade this practice. It was only as a result of the ascetic movement that local churches began to choose men from other places to be bishops. They chose ascetics because they had a reputation as holy men. Even here the community itself chose the man they would accept as their head: bishops were not usually appointed from the outside. The bishops of the fourth century were only applying to ascetic communities the principles that were in operation for all pastoral leaders of the day.

The autonomy of the ascetic community was also respected in the position given to presbyters who became members of ascetic communities subsequent to ordination. The order of the ascetic community and the structure of its leadership was clearly recognized as different from that of the Church at large. Consequently, someone ordained an elder in the Church at large did not immediately begin to function as a leader when he entered an ascetic community. He first became an ordinary member of the community and was formed in its life. Then, if he were the right man within this particular community for the position, he could be chosen as a leader. The early ascetic writers realized the danger that men who had been ordained priests might not be able to relate properly to their new life or to make necessary changes. Here again, the rule of St. Benedict is very explicit:

"If anyone of the priestly order should ask to be received into the monastery, permission shall not be granted him too readily. But if he is quite persistent in his request, let him know that he will have to observe the whole discipline of the rule and that nothing will be relaxed in his favor, that it may be as it is written: 'Friend, for what have you come?'

It shall be granted him, however, to stand next after the abbot and to give blessings and to celebrate mass, but only by order of the abbot. Without such order let him not presume to do anything, knowing that he is subject to the discipline of the rule; but rather let him give an example of humility to all.

If there happens to be question of an appointment or of some business in the monastery, let him expect the rank due him according to the date of his entrance into the monastery, and not the place granted him out of reverence for the priesthood."[144]

In other words, within the ascetic community itself, any consideration rising from ecclesiastical ordination are subordinate to the order of the monastery, except insofar as someone was ordained presbyter to be head of the community.

Once again it is worth pointing out the boldness of the fourth and fifth century bishops. As renewal communities developed rapidly within the ascetic movement, the bishops moved quickly to integrate those communities into the life of the Church. In doing so, they respected the nature of the communities and the order of their life. They did not impose an alien order or an alien leadership, but instead accepted the main lines of the order and life they found and integrated the communities as they were into the life of the local church. One could even say that by the end of our period two pastoral systems existed within the Christian Church, one for Christians who had not undertaken the ascetic life and one for the ascetics. And the pastoral system for the ascetics was directed by ascetics, under the supervision of the bishop. Clearly, an important element in the Church's successful integration of the early ascetic movement was precisely this effort by the bishops to ordain the heads of the ascetic communities and develop good working relationships with them.

V
Renewal Communities
Contribute Leaders

We have discussed two principles for the integration of the ascetic renewal communities into the life of the Church as a whole: the value of unordained elders and the ordination of the heads of ascetic communities. Yet another principle was also important in that process of integration: renewal communities should be drawn upon to make an important contribution to the pastoral strength and the ordained leadership of the Church as a whole. Members of the renewal communities, in other words, should be ordained bishops and priests not just for the service of the renewal communities but also to meet the needs of the Church as a whole.

Communities are not formed primarily to provide services, but to provide a certain kind of life for their members. Yet healthy communities usually have resources that others can draw upon. As the early ascetic communities grew, they became a very fruitful source of pastoral workers for the Church. This is important in itself, because it shows how valuable a renewal movement can be for the Church as a whole. But it is worth noting for another reason as well. The contribution the early ascetic movement made to the pastoral leadership of the Church was an important factor in its successful integration into the Church. Bishops and presbyters who had been part of ascetic communities played a significant role in integrating those communities into the life of the Church. Their experience of ascetic life gave them an understanding of the ascetic communities that enabled them both to provide direction for the ascetics and to draw more skillfully upon the communities for help in the wider Church. Such men were an integrating link between the life of the ascetic movement and the life of the whole Church.

Bishops Encourage Renewal

Many bishops of the fourth and fifth centuries were conscious of the need for renewal in the Church. Even though the Christian Church as the state religion was rapidly achieving a dominant influence in the religious life of the Roman Empire, the Christian people were not always receiving the kind of direction and help they needed and in consequence were often not as fervently Christian as they could have been. While the standard of Christian living still seems to have been somewhat higher than modern standards (this is always a difficult judgment to make), the pastoral leaders of the time felt a need for improvement.

It was not uncommon for bishops of cities throughout the ancient world to look to the new ascetic movement as a source of life for the Church as a whole. From its very beginning some bishops saw the new movement as a potentially helpful source of spiritual influence upon the Christian people and so encouraged the spread of the movement and the foundation of ascetic communities.[145] Athanasius is perhaps the clearest example of a bishop who saw a good thing and encouraged it. He was, in fact, the first to appreciate the value of the ascetic movement for the life of the Church. He wrote to the ascetics, visited them, encouraged them, drew on their support, and even wrote the chief piece of "promotion" for the early ascetic movement (the *Life of Anthony*). Chitty has expressed the importance of his patronage:

"Athanasius, Anthony, Pachomius—bishop and theologian; anchorite; coenobitic abbot . . . the mutual confidence of the three was momentous for their generation in Egypt, and for the universal Church ever since. To it primarily, under God, we owe the integration of monasticism into the Church organism."[146]

Athanasius is best known for his defense of Nicene orthodoxy against the Arians and for his defiance of imperial power to uphold that orthodoxy. But it may be that his greatest accomplishment as a bishop and church statesman was the service he performed in integrating a powerful new and potentially disruptive movement in a positive way into the life of the Church.

Athanasius' example was followed by others.[147] The bishop of Panopolis, a diocese near Pachomius' foundations, invited Pachomius to found a monastery in his diocese "that the blessing of the Lord might come upon our diocese through you." Theophilus, patriarch of Alexandria, constantly encouraged and called upon the ascetics throughout Egypt. In Syria, Walages, bishop of Nisibis, was a great patron of the ascetics and of Ephraem in particular. The bishops of Edessa early took a concern for the development of the ascetic movement in their dioceses, as did other Syrian and Mesopotamian bishops. In Asia Minor, Eustathius, bishop of Sebaste, fostered the growth of ascetic brotherhoods, a work continued by Basil of Caesarea, Gregory Nazianzen, and Gregory of Nyssa. When Chrysostom arrived in Constantinople, he made the growth of ascetic communities an important concern. Sozomen describes his work:

> "He highly commended those who remained in quietude in the monasteries and practiced philosophy [the ascetic life] there; he protected them from all injustice and solicitously supplied whatever necessities they might have."[148]

Ambrose did the same in Milan, particularly encouraging women to become consecrated virgins. Augustine had an important role in encouraging the growth of monasticism in Africa, both before becoming bishop of Hippo and after. Apparently many Gallic bishops, starting with Martin of Tours, took the same strong role. Lazare, the bishop of Aix, seems to have been responsible for Cassian's move to southern Gaul, and Proculus, the bishop of Marseilles, received him. Many other bishops of the area were in active contact with Cassian about the growth of monasticism in their dioceses. Germanus of Auxerre and Vitricius of Rouen were also noted for encouraging the foundation of ascetic communities. A little work on pastoral order written in Gaul in our period, *De septem ordinibus ecclesiae*, urges bishops to gather monks around themselves. In Italy, it was often the bishops who founded ascetic communities, and they seem to have maintained a special relationship with them.

From what we can see, the bishops' patronage of the ascetic communities came from their pastoral concern for their people. They saw the presence of ascetic settlements and communities in their dioceses as a source of Christian life for the people as a whole. There does not seem to have been any expectation that everyone would become part of an ascetic community, but there does seem to have been a common sentiment that strong ascetic communities would lead to a renewal in the spiritual life of the people.

Ascetic Communities Provide Bishops and Presbyters

As the ascetic communities spread throughout the Christian world, often under the direct patronage of the bishops, they began to provide men for the Church who could be good bishops. Wherever the movement penetrated, local churches chose ascetics who impressed them as men of God to be their bishops. Often this choice amounted to a popular rising which carried the new bishop off against his will.

It could not have been much more than twenty-five years after the beginning of our period that the first bishops were chosen for Egyptian dioceses from among the ascetics. Athanasius, in his letter written to Dracontius (c. 354), ascetic-bishop of Hermopolis Parva, names quite a few ascetics who had already been made bishops:

"For you are not the only one who has been elected from among monks, nor the only one to have presided over a monastery, or to have been beloved by monks. But you know that not only was Serapion a monk, and presided over that number of monks; you are not unaware of how many monks Apollos was father; you know Agathon, and are not ignorant of Ariston. You remember Ammonius who went abroad with Serapion. Perhaps you have also heard of Muitus in the upper Thebaid, and can learn about Paul at Latopolis, and many others."[149]

It is likely that the bishopric of Hermopolis Parva, the diocese in which Nitria was situated, was normally filled by ascetics from Nitria. We know that some of Dracontius' successors were also ascetics.[150] Theophilus of Alexandria apparently made a regular practice of ordaining ascetics, and there are early mentions of other monk-bishops.[151]

In Palestine and Syria, the situation was similar.[152] The Syrian church was among the first to draw bishops from the ascetics. Jacob of Nisibis, who died in 338, was possibly one of the earliest. Walages, another early bishop of Nisibis, was a monk drawn from the region of Edessa. Bitos, another monk from Edessa, was the bishop of Harran and Edessa itself had a number of monk-bishops. Barse, bishop in 361, and Rabbula, in the early fifth century, were both monk-bishops of Edessa who have some note. Egeria, on her pilgrimage, mentions a bishop of Edessa who was a monk, as well as another Syrian bishop (the bishop of Batanis) and the bishops of Ramesses in Egypt and of Seleucia in Isauria who were all drawn from the ascetic movement. Abraham, the bishop of Harran and Aqaq, the bishop of Haleb (Beroea) had been ascetics. The list of bishops that Eusebius of Samosata ordained during the reign of the Emperor Valens contains a number of people who had been part of the ascetic movement. The pseudo-Nicene canons, in fact, make it a rule that chorbishops be chosen "from the order of the monks." Within the Persian Empire, Miles, martyred in Susa about 340, is one of the earliest bishops reputed to have been a monk. Subsequent to 375, Aqebsma, the bishop of

Henaita; Aqeblaha and Saborberex, bishops of Karak de Bet Seloh; Barsabba, the missionary of Merv; and the missionary Mar Abdiso were all drawn from the ascetic movement. By 410, at least two of the men who had served as Catholicos (chief bishop in the Empire), Mar Ahai and his successor Jahballaha, had been monks. In Palestine, Epiphanius was elected bishop of Salamis (Cyprus) from his monastery near Jerusalem in 365, John was elected bishop of Jerusalem itself in 386, Porphyry was elected bishop of Gaza about 395, and Netras was elected bishop of Pharan (Sinai) about 400. In Asia Minor,[153] Eustathius of Sebaste was a bishop, and starting in 370 with the consecration of Basil of Caesarea as bishop, many other bishops were drawn from the ascetic movement, including Gregory of Nyssa and Gregory Nazianzen. Gregory Nazianzen was also made patriarch of Constantinople, a position later held by another former ascetic—John Chrysostom. Palladius, the writer of the *Lausiac History*, became a bishop in Hellenopolis in Bithynia in the first years of the fifth century, and the monk Heraclides became bishop of Ephesus about the same time, both by the appointment of Chrysostom.

In the West, the practice was the same.[154] In Africa Augustine of Hippo is an outstanding example, and at least ten of his disciples including Alypius, Evodius, Possidius, Severus, Aurelius, and Profuturus were also made bishops. In Gaul, Martin, who was made bishop in 371, was one of the earliest ascetics. Lerins, an ascetic community in the south of Gaul, was the source of many bishops: Honoratus, the founder, became the bishop of Arles, as did the later monks of Lerins, Hilary and Caesarius. Others include Vitricius of Rouen, Lupus, bishop of Troyes, Maximus and Faustus, bishops of Riez, and Eucharius, bishop of Lyons. These names, however, bring us somewhat outside of our period.

The trend was everywhere the same. The ascetic movement provided more and more bishops for the Church until in some regions (after our period) almost all the bishops were former monks.[155] In many eastern churches, in fact, this is the custom to this day. Moreover, many of those chosen bishops were founders or heads of ascetic communities. A quick look at the above list reveals a number of famous community founders, including Basil of Caesarea, Augustine of Hippo, and Martin of Tours.

Ascetics who became bishops are more often mentioned in our sources because the election of a bishop is more newsworthy. Many more ascetics, however, became presbyters. Basil of Caesarea and Augustine of Hippo were both ordained presbyters before they were consecrated bishops, and there were many other ascetics who served as presbyters. In fact, the bishops' desire to ordain ascetics to the presbyterate was so strong that the Church eventually had to pass laws protecting ascetic communities against bishops who were seeking pastoral helpers.[156]

The number of bishops and presbyters drawn from the ascetic movement shows two things. First of all, it shows the close integration between the ascetic movement and the official leadership of the Church. But it also shows how much the ascetic movement was a source of pastoral strength for the Church. Although the ascetics had a reputation for withdrawal and many of them were reluctant to take on pastoral service, ascetic communities throughout the fourth and fifth centuries increasingly provided pastoral workers for the Church. The pastoral training those workers had received as leaders within the ascetic movement served them well in the larger Church.

Ascetic Communities Provide Other Pastoral Leaders

Earlier, we presented radical social separation as a defining characteristic of the ascetic movement. However, concentrating only on that social separation, or withdrawal, can prevent us from fully understanding the contribution the movement made to the entire Church. More fundamental to the ascetics than withdrawal was their desire to live a full, intense Christian life. More fundamental to the movement than asceticism was its character as a movement of renewal. Like most renewal movements, the ascetic movement also produced a great missionary effort and a major outreach of Christian charity.

The contribution of the ascetic communities was broad. They provided many pastoral workers for the Church: bishops, presbyters, deacons, deaconnesses, missionaries, and teachers. They also made a significant contribution to what we would call social service: help for travelers, relief for the poor, care of orphans, care of the sick, aid to the oppressed, education of all sorts. In describing the ordination of ascetics and bishops and presbyters, some of the pastoral contribution was sketched in. That picture can be filled out with a brief description of the missionary work and the social service that grew out of the ascetic movement.

From the beginning of the movement, there was a strong missionary thrust.[157] Pachomius and his monasteries were outstanding in this regard. A significant number of their members came in through conversion from paganism. The Tabennesiots also once undertook to build a church and evangelize a district at the request of a local bishop. In the conflict with paganism, ascetics took an active part as illustrated by events in the life of Anthony; by an invitation the patriarch of Alexandria made brothers from Scete, asking them to be present at the razing of a pagan temple; and by the settling of a group of Tabennesiot monks on the site of a razed pagan temple.[158] There are also stories of specific missionary endeavors on the part of individual monks. When the two Macarii were exiled to an island during the Arian persecution under Valens, they delivered the daughter of the island's high priest from demon-possession and led the whole tribe to Christianity. When Mavia, the queen of the Saracens, agreed to a treaty with Rome, she stipulated that the anchorite Moses be appointed bishop to her people. He was ordained and sent to the Sacracens and succeeded in converting many of them. A similar story is told of Euthymius in Palestine, who converted a Bedouin tribe and eventually had the chief ordained bishop for his people. Anthony's disciple Hilarion was apparently responsible for much Christian growth in the region near Gaza, largely through his influence as a holy man.

In Syria, Persia, Armenia, and Georgia, missionary efforts were carried on to an even more significant degree.[159] According to

Sozomen, Coele-Syria and Upper Syria (with the exception of Antioch) had been very slow in converting to Christianity. Throughout this region monks settled among the pagans and influenced them toward Christianity, not so much by preaching as by their influence as holy men. In upper Mesopotamia, ascetics often took the lead in missionary work. Abraham Qidunaia was sent about 340 by a bishop to Qidun, a town which had resisted Christianity, and successfully established a Christian congregation. Barse was made bishop of Harran and actively tried to convert it, although without great success. In Syria as in Egypt, the monks took an important part in the destruction of pagan worship. The ascetics also had a significant influence on the Arab tribes. One of the most successful missionaries to the Arabs was Simon Estonaia, the saint who spent much of his life on a pillar. He exercised such fascination for the Arabs that many of them visited him and were converted by his preaching, sometimes whole tribes at once. Inside the non-Christian Persian Empire, ascetics often took the lead in missionary work. Barsabba was missionary to Merw. Mar Abda, a famous ascetic, established a school which trained many successful missionaries. His most famous disciple, Mar Abdiso, evangelized Maisan and Baksaia; part of his strategy was to establish monasteries as centers of evangelization in each area. Jahballaha, who later became Catholicos, was a missionary in Daskarat; he too founded a monastery to carry on the work of evangelization. Petion was missionary to Maisan and Gusnazdad to Hale and Kurdistan. On the coast of Phoenicia, it was mainly monks, sent by John Chrysostom from Constantinople and other provinces, who accomplished the work of conversion. So influential throughout Syria and the bordering countries were the monks that, according to Sozomen, "they were instrumental in leading nearly the whole Syrian nation, and most of the Persians and Saracens, to the proper religion and caused them to cease from paganism."[160]

In the West, the main missionary work of the ascetics happened after our period. The Irish monks evangelized not only Ireland, but much of Scotland, north and west England, and even the continent. Monks sent from Rome under Augustine of Canterbury were responsible for the evangelization of Saxon England. Germany, Scandanavia, and the Slavic lands owed their Christianity to monks, some sent from Western Europe, some sent by the Byzantines. But even during our period, some of the Western ascetics engaged in missionary work. Martin of Tours[161] was one of the most successful missionaries and miracle workers. As bishop of Tours he took bands of co-workers, most of them monks, and converted large numbers of the pagan populace. After his death, some of his followers continued his missionary work. Vitricius did something similar in the area around Rouen.[162]

The ascetic movement provided the same powerful impulse in the field of social service, that it did in missionary work. A great part of this was a natural outgrowth of the life of the monasteries. Where the true ascetic life flourished, two things always happened that had a great social significance. The first was that the ascetics practiced hospitality zealously.[163] Even the hermits would be hospitable if someone came near their cell, to the point of breaking their strictest fasts for the sake of a guest. The welcome that the guests would get from ascetic communities was proverbial. When they arrived in an ascetic community, the monks would vie with one another to receive them. To some degree the hospitality practised by the ascetics was simply the restoration of a social relationship, much as their love for one another was the restoration of a social relationship. But within the ancient world, it was an important contribution towards solving a significant social problem. Traveling in the fourth and fifth centuries was dangerous, and while there were inns, they were not often safe or moral. The ascetics with their hospitality provided badly needed help. As the custom of Christian pilgrimages increased, the hospitality of the ascetics was particularly important. The reception Egeria received from the ascetics and other Christians along her route is one of the more refreshing parts of her story.

A second outgrowth of the ascetics' way of life was care for the poor and needy. While the pattern of life that the ascetics adopted did leave them freer for prayer, it did not stop them from working. In fact, they put a very high value on manual labor and were determined to be productive. Even the hermits worked in their cells. But the ascetics' needs were much less than other men's, since they had no families and led such simple lives. Consequently, they had a great deal to give away. The story of Serapion, the head of all the monks in the district of Arsinoe, shows the results:

"In the season of harvest he would make those who worked for hire from year to year bring and gather together to him twelve ardebs of wheat, that is to say, forty bushels, that it might serve for his ministrations to those in want, and might be distributed by his hands, so that in that district no destitute man might be found, and he sent to the needy in Alexandria the Great their gifts. Now the fathers of whom we have already spoken did not at any time neglect to visit the whole of Egypt, but as a result of the toil of the brethren they used to fill boats with food and apparel, and send them year after year to the poor who were in Alexandria, because the poor and needy who lived around about them were too few to exhaust their benevolence."[164]

Those of us who live in an affluent society do not have a proper consciousness of how important this economic contribution of the ascetics was to people of the fourth century. One of the greatest services a man in the ancient world could perform was to provide for the material needs of people in want. It was a highly valued Christian service, one which compares favorably with any of the activities that go under the name of the lay apostolate today. The ascetics may have chosen work that would not disrupt the pattern of life they had dedicated themselves to, but that did not mean that they did not work hard. Ascetic communities throughout history tended to increase the economic prosperity of the regions they were in. Nor did they work hard for their own welfare only. Basil's instruction was:

"The apostle bids us labor and work with our hands the things which are good, that we may have something to give him that suffers need. It is therefore immediately obvious that we must toil with diligence and not think that our goal of piety offers an escape from work or a pretext for idleness, but occasion for struggle, for ever greater endeavor, and for patience in tribulation . . . Not only is such exertion beneficial for bringing the body into subjection, but also for showing charity to our neighbor in order that through us God may give enough to the weak among our brethren."[165]

Basil's teaching was repeated in much the same vein by most of the other teachers of the ascetic movement.

The contribution the ascetic movement made to the field of social service was not restricted to what happened through the life of the monasteries themselves. The ascetic movement also created a number of institutions, staffed with devoted brothers and sisters from ascetic communities, that met social needs of the day. They not only took in guests themselves, but they established guest houses.[166] The guest house at Alexandria, for instance, was cared for by Isidore, an ascetic. In the Holy Land, many hospices for pilgrims were built and cared for by monks, including Jerome, Rufinus, and Melania. Xenodocheia (guesthouses) staffed by ascetics lined the main pilgrimage routes (for instance, along the routes to Simon Estonaia's pillar) and also many of the important trade routes. Institutions were also established to care for the poor and sick. Macarius, an Egyptian ascetic, was the superior of a hospital for lepers and cripples in Alexandria. Ephraem of Edessa established a hospital for the sick during a famine. Basil set up a hospital in Caesarea for the needy and placed it under the care of the monk Prapidus. Rabbula, the bishop of Edessa, established a similar institution in which the ascetics provided the service. As the fifth century went on, there were probably few cities or traveled places in Mediterranean lands that did not have guesthouses or hospitals staffed by ascetics. In fact, many ascetics seem to have devoted themselves not primarily to prayer but to works of charity, much as many religious orders in recent centuries have.

The social services provided by ascetic communities were very significant. Before the fourth century guests, the needy, and the sick were cared for quite differently by Christians. It was done not by special institutions (we have no evidence that many of these existed) but by the whole Christian people, who would give freely of their possessions and would take people into their homes. The deacons supervised the whole process and ensured that all needs were met to the degree of the available resources. As, during the fourth century, the old social structure of the Christian communities broke down, the diaconate as an effective institution died away and took on a simply liturgical function. That could have left a gap, but precisely at that time a new system was coming into existence: the Christian service institution was created to serve society as a whole (which was rapidly becoming completely Christian). What was needed was people free from the normal responsibilities of family life to staff these institutions, and the ascetic communities took up much of the burden. That is not to say that others did not take part, nor that the old system died away completely (especially in the smaller rural villages). But one characteristic of the Christian Church of the new Christian empire was the presence of either ascetic communities noted for taking in guests and helping the poor, or guesthouses, hospitals and other Christian institutions staffed by ascetic communities.

Other examples of the contribution of the ascetic communities to the work of social welfare in the Church could be described. It is interesting, for example, to see that many ascetics, especially those with some influence, would help the oppressed and individuals (even cities) suffering under some form of social injustice. Or we could study the work of the ascetic communities in education and the place of the monastic schools. But the main point is simply that the ascetic movement was a movement of renewal of Christian life, and it resulted in a general Christian renewal and a renewal of strength among Christian people. Much of that renewal came through the ascetic communities. They were drawn upon to provide many workers and services for the wider Church. Their contribution made their integration into the Church easier, and in turn, the communities' integration into the Church made more feasible the flow of benefits from the communities to the whole Church. What the Church in the Patristic era experienced can be expected from any successful movement or renewal community that is integrated into the life of the Church in a healthy way.

VI
Conclusion

Today within the Catholic Church we are confronted with a new movement for Christian renewal—the charismatic renewal. In many ways, the charismatic renewal has the same sociological character as the early ascetic movement. It is a rapidly growing popular movement that is developing with only an informal structure, and is creating special groups within the Church wanting to live their Christian life differently from the Christians around them. It is a spontaneous response of the Christian spirit to a time when social change and disorganization within the Church have resulted in a loss of fervor among many Christians and a failure of adaptation of the church structure to the changes in its environment. It even has some of the disorderliness that characterized the early ascetic movement and most other informal movements of renewal in their earliest stages. Finally, and most importantly for our purposes, it is giving rise to communities of people who all participate in the movement and who want to live their new life in a more consistent and shared way. There are, of course, differences between the two movements, differences in approach to Christian renewal as well as some differences in sociological form. But the two movements are close enough in character to provide an effective comparison for a study of how renewal communities can and should relate to the larger church.

The renewal communities in the early ascetic movement were integrated into the life of the larger church by an approach that involved three main elements: the use of unordained elders within the renewal communities, the ordination of the head of the community to the presbyterate of the diocese in which the community was situated, and the use by the wider church of ordained bishops and presbyters and other Christian workers drawn from the renewal communities. These three elements formed one system. The unordained elders provided an appropriate leadership system for the emerging renewal communities. The fact that they were not ordained allowed a greater flexibility in the relationship of the renewal communities to the structure of the whole church. The ordination of the head of the community provided the main structural link between the leadership system of the renewal community and the leadership system of the church as a whole. It was viewed as the normal and most appropriate way to establish that link and not as something that was done primarily to provide a sacramental ministry. There are other ways of providing a sacramental ministry. Finally, the use of capable people from the renewal communities as ordained (and unordained) workers in the wider church both provided a way for the stronger integration of the communities into the whole church and provided a way for the renewal communities to serve the rest of the church. Together these three elements made up a successful system of integration of the renewal communities into the wider church, a system that we should consider both because of its previous effectiveness and because it was the solution offered in the patristic era to one of our needs.

In order to use the approach of the church in the fourth and fifth centuries, there would have to be some changes in the current pastoral approach of the Catholic Church. The use of unordained elders presents few problems. While the title is not common, the position and function is. As long as the "unordained elders" that are currently serving in the renewal communities are in good relationship with their bishops, they are taking a traditional Catholic role, not presenting a sectarian danger. Their wider acceptance is mainly a matter of growing trust between the renewal communities and the church. Drawing upon people from the renewal communities to fill ordained positions in the wider church also presents few problems. If the renewal communities that are growing out of the charismatic renewal are effective as communities, people within them will be recognized for their pastoral ability, and the church will be eager to use them. If there is any problem it will probably be a difficulty in reconciling the demands upon the same group of people that come from the needs of the renewal communities and the demands that come from the needs of the wider church.

The ordination of the heads of the renewal communities, however, would involve more of a change in the current approach. It is, to be sure, not essential that the heads of the renewal communities be ordained for integration into the life of the church to happen successfully. Sacramental ministry can be obtained other ways, either by having a priest within the community taking a "chaplain" role and providing sacramental services without being one of the heads of the community or by the community going outside of itself when its needs are sacramental. There are examples of both in the early ascetic movement. The proper relationship between the authority of the bishop and the renewal community can also be worked out in other ways. As long as some regular relationship is worked out between the bishop and the head or heads of the community, the head does not have to be ordained. Again, there are examples in the early ascetic movement of many renewal communities that were peacefully integrated into the life of the wider church without the ordination of their heads. Yet, the instinct of the patristic church, especially of the bishops, asserted itself strongly in favor of ordaining the heads of communities as the normal way.

The bishops in the patristic era wanted to ordain the heads of the renewal communities to the presbyterate for three reasons. One reason came from their understanding of the presbyterate. Since the presbyterate (priesthood) is a governing office, it is appropriate for those who are governing Christian people to be ordained presbyters. It is less appropriate for a presbyter to be performing simply sacramental functions under someone who is not an ordained presbyter. A second reason came from their understanding of community. As was discussed above, the whole patristic age had an instinct for the principle that a community ought normally to choose its own leaders rather than to have its leaders assigned to it by someone outside of the community. There also seems to be a third reason, one which cannot be documented readily from the sources. The desire of the bishops in the patristic era to ordain the heads of the renewal communities to the presbyterate seems to have involved a desire to link them as fully to the diocese as possible. Ordination of the head of the community to the bishop's presbyterate tied him directly and officially to the headship of the local church. Underlying such a procedure must have been a vision of the relationship of renewal community and diocese that must have been more organic than the relationship other approaches would provide.

There are difficulties in the way of applying the patristic approach to the current situation of charismatic communities. Some of those difficulties come from the new and untried nature of both the charismatic renewal and the charismatic communities. Before a closer relationship can develop, there will have to be greater maturity and more trust between bishops and renewal members. Many of those difficulties, however, come from the lay character of the charismatic communities. Within the charismatic communities, the heads are commonly chosen as the need arises because of their ability to do the job. They often have not been trained for ordination nor could they be spared for four years at a seminary. That does not mean that they are untrained for pastoral service nor that they are uneducated theologically. They often are capable in building community and caring for people, and they often have as much theological understanding as the normal parish priest. In order for the patristic approach to work in regard to the current charismatic communities, a somewhat different approach to the training of those to be ordained than the current seminary system would have to be found. That approach would probably have to be something that could be built into the ongoing life of the charismatic communities.[167]

This study has not yet raised directly the further issue of normativeness in matters of pastoral practice. One norm that could be used is the pragmatic norm: "if it works, do it." Much can be said in favor of the pragmatic norm. We should at least accept it to the degree that we should be willing to say: "if it is causing trouble, don't do it." On the grounds of the pragmatic norm, the patristic approach proved its effectiveness in the past and looks like a promising approach for the present. Nonetheless, the pragmatic norm is not adequate for a Christian. Our concern is not simply to come up with something that works. Our concern is to be the body of Christ in the world, and we therefore have to be concerned with how Christ wants his body to be shaped.

There are a variety of commonly used norms in pastoral thinking today: e.g., biblical teaching, current church practice, adaptation to the world. A consideration of the various norms and how they should be applied goes beyond the scope of the present study. However, it is appropriate to recall that the teaching and practice of the great Fathers of the Church have always held a place in Catholic teaching second in authority only to the Scripture itself and to subsequent canonical pronouncements of the Universal Church. If the fathers do have such a position, their solution to the pastoral situation we are facing ought to be considered with special seriousness.

ABBREVIATIONS KEY

ACW—*Ancient Christian Writers*, the works of the Fathers in translation, ed. J. Quasten and J.C. Plumpe.

CSCO—Corpus Scriptorum Christianorum Orientalium

CSEL—Corpus Scriptorum Ecclesiasticorum Latinorum

Ep. Am.—*Epistula Ammonis* (ed. Halkin, *Sancti Pachomii Vitae Graecae*, Subsidia Hagiographica 19, Brussels, 1932.)

FCS—The Fathers of the Church Series

G. Mac. Aeg.—sayings of Macarius of Egypt in the Alphabetical Gerontikon (in *Patrologia Graeca*, 65, 71-440.)

H.E.—*Historia Ecclesiastica* (of Sozomen, Socrates, Eusebius)

H.L.—Lausiac History

H.M.—*Historia Monachorum in Aegypto*

PG—*Patrologia Graeca* (ed. Migne)

PL—*Patrologia Latina* (ed. Migne)

RAM—*Revue d'Ascetique et de Mystique*

SA—Studia Anselmiana

SLNF—Select Library of the Nicene Fathers.

Soc.—Socrates (*Historia Ecclesiastica*)

Soz.—Sozomen (*Historia Ecclesiastica*)

TSt—Texts and Studies

T-U—Texte und Untersuchungen zur Geschichte der Altchristlichen Literatur

V.B.Bo.—*Vita Bachomi Bohairica* (ed. Lefort, CSCO)

V.B.G.—*Vita Bachomi Graeca* (ed. Halkin)

V.S.—Verbum Seniorum (PL 73, 355-1022)

NOTES

1. The distinction is found in Ernst Troeltsch's *The Social Teaching of the Christian Churches* (New York: Macmillan, 1931). The distinction has been used often since Troeltsch and is a useful one. As Troeltsch elaborated it, however, it only applies to a situation of a "Christian society" where there is a dominant church that most people belong to and smaller Christian sects. When the Lutheran and Catholic Churches find themselves in situations where they are a small minority in a non-Christian society, they begin to look more like what Troeltsch calls sects than churches.

2. Defining what is one movement can be difficult. Sometimes we want to call the whole movement associated with the mendicant orders and Innocent III one movement (something like "the evangelical movement of the high middle ages") and trace its lineage to figures like Robert of Arbrissel and Peter Waldo, and even to the Cistercians. Sometimes we want to consider it a number of movements (the Franciscan movement, the Dominican movement, the crusader movements, etc.).

3. Stephen B. Clark, *Building Christian Communities* (Notre Dame, Ind.: Ave Maria, 1972) pp. 146-172.

4. For a description of the new emerging communities in the charismatic renewal, see Ralph Martin, "Life in Community" and Bert Ghezzi, "Three Charismatic Communities," *As the Spirit Leads Us*, ed. Kevin and Dorothy Ranaghan (Paramus, New Jersey: Paulist Press, 1971).

5. Michael Harper, *A New Way of Living* (Plainfield, New Jersey: Logos International, 1973).

6. I have deliberately chosen the term "ascetic movement" rather than "monastic movement," because for most people today, the term "monastic" is synonymous with "coenobitic" and carries heavily institutional connotations.

7. Perhaps a more precise way of saying this is: the ascetic movement was a "safe" example to choose among Catholics until recently. In the last decades, particularly since the beginning of the Vatican Council, many Catholic writers have been more negative on the ascetic movement (as on everything else "Catholic"). For some reflections on this problem, see p. 97.

8. Georges Florovsky, "Empire and Desert: Antinomies of Christian History," *Cross Currents* IX 3 (Summer, 1959), p. 244.

9. Most of the articles or books which take a pastoral perspective on the ascetic movement or deal with questions of structure and leadership in a helpful way can be found in the second section of the bibliography.

10. A recent discussion in the area is the discussion on the priesthood of monks. Very few of the articles that enter into the discussion take a clearcut pastoral perspective (asking how leadership arrangements functioned in people's lives). For a good treatment of the question, see Jean Leclercq, "The Priesthood for Monks," *Monastic Studies* 3 (1965), pp. 51-64.

11. There are many roles of leadership among the Christian people (e.g., prophets, catechists, songleaders are all Christian "leaders"). Among those, some have been established as "heads" of the people. "Heads" are those who have the overall responsibility for the Christian people as a whole or for sections of them. They are the ones who "govern" their lives. Bishops and presbyters are heads of the people as a whole. Fathers are heads of their families. Abbots are heads of their monasteries.

12. The term "shepherd" was applied in the Old Testament to the rulers of the Israelite people (Jer. 2:8; Ezek. 34:1-6). In the New Testament, the term was applied to the elders or presbyters (Acts 20:28-29; 1 Peter 5:2-4). There is some evidence that the term was primarily applied to the bishop by some groups of Christians in the first few centuries. "Pastor" is the Latin word for "shepherd" and has been taken over into English. "Pastor" or "pastoral" are nowadays commonly (and quite loosely) used of anyone in the Church who has a significant responsibility for the Christian nurturance of others.

13. Deacons and deaconesses in the early Church were not heads of the Church or pastors. As assistants of the bishop, functioning under his direction, they performed pastoral or governing

functions, but those functions were performed as extensions of the bishop. The functions of the deacon have changed considerably over the centuries to the point where now it might be reasonable to consider them as directly sharing in the headship of the Church, especially those who are being ordained to the new permanent diaconate, who function more like presbyters who have limitations on their authority than like the deacons of the early Church. For a good discussion of deacons in the early Church, see Jean Colson, "Diakon und Bischof in den ersten drei Jahrhunderten der Kirche" pp. 23-30. and Walter Croce, "Aus der Geschichte des Diakon-ates," in *Diaconia in Christo* (Freiburg: Herder, 1962), pp. 92-128. For a modern description of the role of the deacon, see the Constitution on the Church of the second Vatican Council, section 29.

14. For the significance of Chalcedon and its place in the de-velopment of monasticism in its relationship to the Church (espe-cially structurally), see Leo Ueding, "Die Kanones von Chalkedon in ihrer Bedeutung fur Mönchtum and Klerus," *Das Konzil von Chalkedon* (Würzburg: Echter-Verlag, 1953), pp. 569-676. For the revolutionary change in the situation which was involved in the rise of religious orders, see David Knowles, *From Pachomius to Igna-tius* (Oxford: Clarendon Press, 1966).

15. Some of the classic works taking this approach are Adolph Von Harnack, *Monasticism: Its Ideals and History* (Lon-don: Williams and Norgate, 1901); Richard Reitzenstein, *Historia Monachorum und Historia Lausica* (Göttingen, 1916); Herbert Workman, *The Evolution of the Monastic Ideal* (Boston: Beacon Press, (1963) 1913 Karl Heussi, *Der Ursprung des Mönchtums* :(Tübingen: Mohr, 1936). The approach is founded more on a philosophical view (Idealist) of the opposition of spirit and in-stitution than on factual evidence, as is commonly recognized. The approach has a remarkable tenacity. Some modern examples are E. Amandd de Mendieta, "Le système cénobitique basilien comparé au système cénobitique pachômien," *Revue de l'histoire des religions* 152 (1957); Thomas M. Gannon and George W. Traub, *The Desert and the City* (New York: Macmillan, 1969). It is remarkable to see modern Catholic writers so influenced by someone like Workman the way Gannon and Traub are. For good critiques of some aspects of the approach, see Henrich Bacht, "Die Rolle des orientalischen Mönchtums in den kirchen-

politischen Auseinandersetzungen um Chalkedon," *Das Konzil von Chalkedon* (Würzburg: Echter-Verlag, 1953), pp. 229-307; and Armand Veilleux, *La liturgie dans le cénobitisme pachômien au quatrième siècle*, Studia Anselmiana 57 (1968), pp. 189-195.

16. There seems to be a school of sorts developing which is based upon solid historical investigation into the early ascetic movement and which is presenting the early ascetic movement precisely as a movement of Christian renewal. Among the foremost figures in this school would be men like Bacht, Gribomont, De Vogue, and Veilleux (see bibliography). In addition, the trend of the solidest scholarship in the area (among Christians at least) seems to be moving in this direction.

17. For a fuller description of the early ascetic movement as a broad, popular movement, see Bacht, "Die Rolle," pp. 292-296.

18. The best survey of the development of the early ascetic movement in Egypt and Palestine is to be found in Derwas J. Chitty, *The Desert a City: An Introduction to the Study of Egyptian and Palestinian Monasteries Under the Christian Empire* (Oxford: Basil Blackwell, 1966).

19. For a discussion of the recent research and views in the area, see Armand Veilleux, "The Abbatial Office in Cenobitic Life," *Monastic Studies* 6 (1968): 5-15.

20. See Arthur Vöobus, *A History of Asceticism in the Syrian Orient* (Louvain: CSCO, 1958, 1960), for a description of the growth of the Syrian ascetic movement.

21. Chitty, *The Desert*, pp. 13-16.

22. Jean Gribomont, "Le monachisme au IVe siècle en Asie Mineure: de Gangres au messalianisme," *Studia Patristica*, vol. 2 (Berlin: TU Vol. 64, 1957).

23. The growth of the ascetic movement in the East is described in Vöobus, *History*, vol. 1, vol. 2: pp. 353-360; Chitty, *The Desert*, pp. 82-181; Bacht, "Die Rolle," p. 295.

24. The growth of the ascetic movement in the West is described in Chitty, *The Desert*, Chapter 3; John Ryan, *Irish Monastivism* (Ithaca, N.Y.: Cornell University Press, 1972); Élie Griffe, "Saint Martin et le monachisme gaulois," *Studia Anselmiana* 46 (1961): 3-24.

25. At the Council of Ephesus for the first time. Cf. Eduard

Schwartz, *Acta conciliorum oecumenicorum* (Berlin: Walter de Gruyter, 1914). Also, Vöobus, *History*, 2: p. 204.

26. Canons 4, 6, 7, 8, 16, 18, 23, and 24 of the Council of Chalcedon. There are other canons earlier (e.g., the pseudo-Nicene canons or the African code), but Chalcedon marked the first time that an ecumenical council explicitly legislated for monastic life.

27. Vöobus, *History*, 1: pp. 150-156, 2: pp. 19-41; Frederick Holmes Dudden, *Gregory the Great* (New York: Russell & Russell, 1905) pp. 346-7.

28. John Cassian, *Conferences*, 2:5-7, 18:7-8, 19:10-11 (to choose just a few examples).

29. Palladius, *The Lausiac History*, trans Robert T. Meyer (Westminister, Md.: Newman Press, 1965) ACW, vol. 34, pp. 25-28.

30. The innovative and distinctive aspects of the spirituality of the ascetic movement are discussed in most histories of spirituality. The teaching on interpersonal relationships, however, is rarely treated as a topic in itself. Some of the innovative elements of the movement's teaching on interpersonal relations are found in the picture drawn of the character of the ideal Christian (in which humility, obedience, patience, and self-control receive more central roles than in earlier teaching), the encouragement to limit normal social interrelating (*eg.* through strictures on unnecessary speech and laughter) rather than to use it as a means of growth, and the shift in the focus of concern from the developing of good relationships to the formation of the inner life of the individual. Many of the ascetic movement's teachings in these areas have been criticized in recent attempts to create a "contemporary" or "lay" spirituality. The value of the ascetic movement's teaching is not to the point. The distinctiveness of it, however, is important for our purposes.

31. For a clear treatment of this point, see Cassian *Conferences*, 3.

32. The form of the definition is my own. For the elements and the how they are found in early ascetic writers, see Garcia M. Colombas, "The Ancient Concept of the Monastic Life," *Monastic Studies* 2 (1964), pp. 65-118.

33. For the same approach, see Georges Florovsky, "Empire

and Desert: Antinomies of Christian History," p. 244.

34. Cf. the reference in note 19.

35. Chitty, *The Desert*, chapter 1, especially p. 9.

36. A social movement is a special environment resulting from the voluntary interaction among committed advocates for change in the patterning of society or of a grouping in society. See Clark, *Building Christian Communities*, p. 152.

37. This would be, for instance, Chitty's approach to describing the origin of the movement in chapter 1 of *The Desert*.

38. Colombas, Ancient Concept," p. 97.

39. Veilleux, "Abbatial Office," p. 11.

40. Peter Munz, "John Cassian," *The Journal of Ecclesiastical History* XI (1960) I, p. 2.

41. *Ibid.*, p. 3.

42. John Chrysostom *Contra oppugnatores vitae monasticae* III. 14.

43. Basil *The Long Rules* 1-6.

44. Athanasius *The Life of Anthony* c. 2-3.

45. *Verba Seniorum* II. 3.

46. *V.P. G. (Vita Pachomi Graeca)* c. 23; *V.P.Bo. (Vita Pachomi Bohairica)* c. 22.

47. See Clark, *Baptized in the Spirit*. (Pecos, Dove Public., 1970), pp. 44-50.

48. Gribomont, "Le Monachisme au IVe Siècle" p. 404.

49. *V.P.Bo.* 194. For a treatment of the "return to early Christian community" in Pachomius and his followers, see Veilleux, *La liturgie*, pp. 176-181.

50. Basil *Long Rules* 7.

51. Augustine *Sermons 355 and 356*.

52. Augustine *On the Psalms* Ps. 133.

53. Cassian *Institutes* II. 5.

54. Cassian *Conferences* XVIII, 5.

55. Colombas, "Ancient Concept," p. 107.

56. For a discussion of when special communities form within a larger social grouping see Clark, *Building Christian Communities*, pp. 40-46.

57. Eusebius of Caesarea *Ecclesiastical History* VIII, 1.

58. Most sizable church histories have a discussion of the for-

mation of the parish system during this period. See, for example, Karl Baus, "From the Apostolic Community to Constantine," in *Handbook of Church History*, ed. Hubert Jedin and John Dolan (New York: Herder and Herder, 1965) vol. 1, pp. 349, 380; Henri Marrou, *The Christian Centuries*, ed. L. Rogier, D. Knowles, et al. (New York: McGraw-Hill, 1969) vol. 1, part 2, pp. 219-220, 297, 391.

59. Socrates *Historia Ecclesiastica* 5, 19; Sozomen *Historia Ecclesiastica* 7, 16; for a description of the change see Bernhard Poschmann, *Penance and the Anointing of the Sick* (New York: Herder and Herder, 1964) pp. 81-2, 98-9, 123.

60. For a description of the change, see Croce, "Aus der Geschichte des Diakonates."

61. Veilleux, *La liturgie*, p. 186.

62. Gribomont, "Le monachisme en Asie Mineure," pp. 408-414.

63. The word "monastery" originally meant the dwelling place of a "monos" (monk), a solitary. The most primitive meaning of the word, the one used in this passage, is the cell of a monk, which normally would be a small building just large enough for one person (or at times a small group) to live in. Later on, as coenobia became the prevalent form of monasticism in most regions, the word "monastery" came to refer to a large building or complex of buildings that was built to house many monks.

64. The early ascetics in Egypt would often settle in deserted Pagan temples.

65. *Historia Monachorum in Aegypto* 5.

66. *H.L.* 7; see also, *H.M.* 21; Soz. *H.E.* VI, 31.

67. *H.L.* 18; *H.M.* 22, Soz *H.E.* VI, 31; Cassian *Conferences* VI,1.

68. Cassian *Conferences* III, 1; X, 2.

69. Egeria, *Diary of a Pilgrimage*, trans. George E. Gingras (New York: Newman Press, 1970), c. 3, 20, 23.

70. Veilleux, *La liturgie*, pp. 166-171.

71. Chitty, *The Desert*, pp. 15-16.

72. Cyril of Scythopolis *Vita Euthymii* 9, 16. ed. Schwartz, *Kyrillos von Skythopolis*, TU vol. 49 (2), 1939 pp. 3-84.

73. Cyril of Scythopolis *Vita Sabas* 28. (TU Vol. 49 (2) 1939) pp. 85-200.

74. Possidius, *Vita Augustini*; Augustine *Sermons* 355 and 356; Augustine, *Rule* translated by T.A. Hand. Westminster, Md., Newman Press, 1956.

75. Basil *The Long Rules* and *The Short Rules*; Soc. *H.E.* IV 26; Soc. *H.E.* VI, 1.

76. Ambrose *Letters* 63.

77. Soz. *H.E.* VI 31.

78. Paulinus *Letters* 15:4, 23:8, 27:2.

79. Augustine *De moribus ecclesiae catholicae* 31, 70-73.

80. Leclerc, "The Priesthood for Monks," pp. 58-68.

81. "Another indication (to which we must grow accustomed because it is rather different from what we normally expect) is that priesthood was not then, as it is now, necessary for the ministry of souls. First, it was not necessary to be a priest in order to preach: we see many saintly monks and hermits preaching without, or before, being ordained to the priesthood; and this is sometimes clearly specified, as in the life of St. Ansbert. Secondly, it was not necessary to be a priest in order to exercise spiritual paternity. In the life of St. Ansbert again, we read that after he had been ordained a priest, he heard sacramental confessions. Let us notice that these words speak of the fact as of an exception, something which deserves special mention since it distinguishes this monk from the others as a group." LeClercq, "On Monastic Priesthood, According to the Ancient Medieval Tradition," *Studia Monastica*, Vol. III, fasc. I (1961) pp. 137-155.

82. *H.L.* 12, 17, 18, 35, 36; *H.M.* 2, 16, 20; *Vita Antoni*, 60-64.

83. See Veilleux, *La liturgie*, pp. 189-190 for a discussion of how charismatic authority operated in the pastoral position of St. Pachomius. His discussion is marred by a modern tendency to equate the role of prophet with any charismatic or non-institutional function of leadership (as in "monks should be prophets in the church today"), but the discussion is helpful.

84. Athanasius *Life of Anthony*, especially c. 67.

85. *V.P.Bo.* 25, 28.

86. Among many accounts of unordained elders teaching authoritatively, the following are interesting: Athanasius *Life of Anthony* 15-43 (Anthony's system of teaching and a discourse); Jerome *Vita S. Hilarionis* 14, 25 (Hilarion's approach to teaching);

H.M. 7, 11 (accounts of Apollos of Hermopolis and Helenus and their teaching).

87. The writings in the monastic literature about obedience all concern pastoral direction of ascetics, and much of this was done by the unordained elders.

88. For a description of penance in the Pachomian monasteries, see Veilleux, *La liturgie*, pp. 353-358. See also, the Pachomian rules: *Praecepta* 151, 152, 153, 154, 158, 180 and *Praecepta atque Iudicia*.

89. Basil *The Long Rules* 38, 47.

90. Benedict *Rule* 23-30.

91. For a discussion of the question, see Veilleux, *La liturgie*, pp. 358-364.

92. For a summary discussion of the relationships between the church authorities and these men, see Bacht, "Die Rolle," pp. 297-307.

93. *V.P.Bo.* 58; see Veilleux, *La liturgie*, p. 353.

94. *V.S.* IV. 12, 21; VI. 8, 9; Benjamin 2; *H.L.* 18, 25.

95. Cassian *Conferences* X, 2.

96. *H.L.* 7.

97. Cassian *Conferences* II; III. 1; IV. 1; X. 2, 3. See De Vogue's discussion of Cassian's view of the ascetic community as a local church in Adalbert De Vogue, "Monasticism in the Church in the Writings of Cassian," *Monastic Studies* 3 (1965): 44-47.

98. Cassian *Conferences* IV. 1, X. 2, 3.

99. *Ibid.*, II; XIV. 9; XVIII. 3; XIX, 1.

100. *Ibid.*, II. 10-13; IV. 20 et passim.

101. The role of the unordained elders in penitential discipline is not completely lacking in Cassian's view of Scete, but it is not prominent in the way he sketches their function. The presbyters seem to take a more active role. See Cassian *Conferences* XVIII, 15.

102. *V.S.* V. 27, 34; IX. 2, 9; X. 18, 110; Daniel 7; Isaac 1. See also *H.L.* 25.5 and possibly 26.2. Dörries has an article "The Place of Confession in Ancient Monasticism," *Studia Patristica* V (Berlin: TU Vol. 80, 1962): 284-311, which is helpful in understanding early ascetic "spiritual direction," but which is misleading in significant ways. He centers on some sayings in the *Apophthegmata*

which are negative towards the traditional penitential discipline. They seem to stem from the circle of Abba Poemen, who in different ways exhibits an untraditional, unscriptural anti-structuralism. Dörries neglects (for a purpose) the normal approach to the area as exhibited in the above references, and hence conveys the sense that the early ascetic movement did not practice a penitential discipline.

103. *V.S.* III. 9; VI. 7; VII. 44; X. 109; XV. 8 (also preserved as Arsenius 16), 21; Cronius 5; Isaac 1; Macarius 26; Motius 2. The saying preserved in Macarius 26 is particularly interesting, because it contains an account of how Macarius went to consult Anthony about the situation in Scete, and upon receiving Anthony's advice that what was needed was a regular Eucharist, returned to lay the advice before the council of elders who deliberated on how to change the situation.

104. In the Pachomian *Regulae*, each of the individual monasteries is headed by a *pater monasterii*. Each of the houses (about 40 monks) is headed by a *praepositus*. The rules also refer to elders *(maiori)*: 8, 11, 17, 18, 19, 30, 31, 51, 61, 96, 112, 137, 146, 150, 155, 170, and 179. They seem to be a recognized group of men who take responsibility for the life together in different ways. Whether we consider the *praepositi* or the *maiori* as well, the Pachomian coenobia had a recognized group of unordained elders.

105. The fullest discussion that I know about the "unordained elders" in Basil's coenobia is in William Kemp Lowther Clarke, *The Ascetic Works of St. Basil* (New York: Macmillan, 1925), pp. 39-42. His views have been debated since then, but the section referred to gives all the main references, the Greek vocabulary, and a sound, if controversial, view of the area. How unordained elders function in Basil's coenobia is not clear.

106. Basil, *Short Rules* 235.

107. Benedict *Rule*, especially c. 3, 4, 63, 71.

108. See note 15 above. The relations between bishops and ascetics were not, of course, always problem-free. Problems in relationships and denial of authority are, however, two different matters.

109. It is not always possible to tell from the English translation what the original Greek or Latin term was. Often English

translators will use the word "priest" to translate the Greek *presbuteros* or the Latin *presbyter*. The term "priest" *(hiereus, sacerdos)* began to be commonly applied to the Christian bishop as a title towards the end of the second century and the beginning of the third, and to all the Christian ordained presbyters in the middle of the fourth century. To my knowledge, it is never used as a title of someone who has not been ordained.

110. In many translations of ascetic literature, the word *geron* is translated "old man." While it is a linguistically accurate translation, it does not convey that sense of a special role and position which the word "elder" does and which the word *geron* was used to designate. Cassian treats the question in *Conferences* 13.2, distinguishing between those who are *seniores* by age and those who are *seniores* by position. The discussion indicated a non-formalized position, but a real one nonetheless.

111. The word *senior* was used at times to refer to ordained elders (e.g., in Tertullian and Cyprian), but from early on, the word *presbyter* was the normal title.

112. See Colombas, "Ancient Concept," pp. 106-7 for a brief summary. See Adalbert De Vogue, "Le Monastère, Église du Christ," in *Commentationes in Regulam S. Benedicti*, ed. Basilius Steidle, *Studia Anselmiana* 42 (Rome: Herder, 1957), pp. 25-46, for a longer discussion.

113. Veilleux, *La liturgie*, pp. 181-182.

114. *Ibid.*, p. 353.

115. Basil *Long Rules* 7, 24, 28, 47.

116. Benedict *Rule* 5, 28.

117. When renewal communities that have grown out of the charismatic renewal have done something similar, they have, at times, been accused of modeling themselves on (or being influenced by) the Protestant "Believers Church" (the Anabaptist tradition). In fact, their approach is much closer to that taken by the early ascetic communities, who neither denied the authority of the hierarchy or order of the Church as a whole, nor separated themselves from communion with the Church as a whole nor obedience to its bishops. For a theological discussion of precisely this issue, see Adalbert De Vogue, "Monasticism and the Church in the Writings of Cassian," *Monastic Studies* 3 (1965): 30-31, 42-51;

and Veilleux, *La liturgie*, pp. 181-189. See also articles mentioned in note 105.

118. For a summary of the ordination of the heads of ascetic communities to the presbyterate, see Bacht, "Die Rolle," pp. 301-2.

119. *V.P.G.* 26, 30; *V.P.Bo.* 38.

120. *G. Mac. Aeg.* 2; *Ep Am.* c. 32; *H.L.* 17, 18; Soz. *H.E.* III. 14; Cassian *Conferences* III. 1, XVIII. 15, IV. 1.

121. Cassian, *Conferences*, iv, 1. Macarius of Egypt made a similar attempt to establish a successor in his disciple John. *HL* xvii.

122. *H.L.* 58; Cassian *Conferences* XVIII. 1; *H.L.* 47.

123. *H.M.* 3, 10, 13, 15.

124. *H.L.* 44, 46.

125. Jerome *Letters* LI.

126. Egeria *Pilgrimage* 3, 15.

127. *H.L.* 48, 49.

128. Canon 6 of Council of Chalcedon.

129. Cyril of Scythopolis *Vita Sabas* c. 19-20.

130. Some instances of this usage: *V.S.* IV. 12, 21, 55; VII. 14, XI. 17; Benjamin 2, Eulogius 1, Isidore 1, Isaac 1, Pambo 11, *H.L.* 12.1, 18.1, 44.1; Cassian *Conferences* III.1, XVIII.1, 15. These references are by no means exhaustive, but are representative of the literature concerning subject.

131. *H.L.* 48, Basil *Letters* 24, 291. "Chorbishop" was the title given primarily in the East to the bishop of a country district. Limited to caring for those in rural and village areas, he was subject to the authority of the bishop in his region and restricted in his exercise of episcopal powers. For a description of the development of chorbishops, see p. 54.

132. Soz. *H.E.* VI. 34.

133. Workman, and Gannon and Traub following him, talk about the "protest of the lay spirit" against ordination and clericalization. Workman is clearly reading back the "protest of the lay spirit" that existed in nineteenth century Europe into the early ascetic movement. Although the early ascetic movement was a lay movement (a movement of the Christian people), not a clerical movement, it did not exhibit a "lay spirit" of protest. Athanasius'

letter is one of the clearest refutations of this view.

134. Athanasius *Ad Dracontium* 10.

135. For a survey of how the position operated, see Bacht, "Die Rolle," pp. 296-299. See also, Chitty, *The Desert*, pp. 84, 86, 110.

136. *H.M.* 18.

137. See note 53.

138. For a description of the administration of the penitential discipline and the role of the presbyter in it during our period, see Poschmann, *Penance*, pp. 97-99.

139. Cassian *Conferences* IV. 1.

140. See Leclercq, "The Priesthood for Monks," pp. 58-68.

141. Benedict *Rule* 62. The councils of Arles (455), Agde (506), Lerida (524), and Carthage (536) insisted on the abbot's permission for the ordination of one of his monks.

142. See Clark, *Building Christian Communities*, pp. 134-145.

143. *Ibid.*, pp. 33-40.

144. Benedict *Rule* 160.

145. There were, of course, a fair number of bishops at the beginning who were reserved or even hostile about the growth of the ascetic movement. By the end of the fourth century, few if any remained who were not positive.

146. Chitty, *The Desert*, p. 1.

147. *V.P.Bo.* c. 55; Bacht, "Die Rolle," p. 297; Vöobus, *History*, 2: pp. 86-7, 161-2; Augustine *Confessions* VII. 6-15; Sulpicius Severus *The Life of Martin* 13; see Griffe's view in "Saint Martin," pp. 12-13; Cassian *Institutes* preface; *Conferences* prefaces to each part; Griffe, "Saint Martin," p. 18; Ueding, "Die Kanones," pp. 598-9; Paulinus of Nola *Letters* 18. 4, 5.

148. Soz. *H.E.* VII. 9.

149. Athanasius *Ad Dracontium* 7.

150. *H.L.* 12.

151. Palladius *Dialogue on the Life of John Chrysostom* 17; Cassian *Conferences* XI. 2.

152. Vöobus, *History*, 2: pp. 119, 88, 330; Egeria *Pilgrimage* 8, 19, 20, 23; Vöobus, *History*, 2: pp. 15, 119; 1: pp. 242, 249, 263-

5, 269; Soz. *H.E.* VII. 32; Chitty, *The Desert*, pp. 71-2.

153. Soz. *H.E.* III. 14; Soc. *H.E.* 26; Soz. *H.E.* VI. 16; Soc. *H.E.* IV. 27, VIII 2; Soz. *H.E.* VI. 3; *H.L.* 35; Chitty, *The Desert*, p. 59.

154. Soz. *H.E.* VIII. 6; Possidius *Vita Augustini* 10, 11; Paulinius of Nola, Ep. 32:1; Sulpicius Severus *Vita Martini* 9; Hilary of Arles *Sermo de vita s. Honorati*; Paulinus of Nola *Letters* 18; Ryan, *Irish Monasticism*, p. 56.

155. Bacht, "Die Rolle," pp. 302-03.

156. Ueding, "Die Kanones," pp. 575-6, 599-600.

157. Veilleux, *La liturgie*, pp. 198-206; Athanasius *Vita Antoni* 46, 68-71; *V.S.* IV. 63; Chitty, *The Desert*, p. 47; Soc. *H.E.* IV. 24, 36; Soz. *H.E.* VI. 38, III. 14; Chitty, *The Desert*, p. 83; Jerome, *Vita Hilarionis*. Often "missionary" did not mean going to a foreign country. Sometimes it did not involve active efforts to reach new people but rather preaching to those who came. Still, in the broad sense of "missionary," the ascetic movement had a substantial missionary thrust.

158. Missionary efforts during the first century of the Christian empire involved a fair amount of active destruction of paganism.

159. Vöobus, *History*, 2: pp. 56-7, 15, 348-9, 344-48, 320-2; 1: pp. 310-15, 230-1, 263, 266f, 270-1, 290-4; 2: pp. 342-3.

160. Soz. *H.E.* VI. 34.

161. Sulpicius Severus *Vita Martini* 13.

162. Paulinus *Letters* 18. 4, 5.

163. *V.S.* XII. 1, 4, 7, 10; Cassian *Institutes* V. 24-7; *H.M.* 8, 23; Benedict *Rule* 53.

164. *H.M.* 29.

165. Basil *Long Rules* 37.

166. *H.L.* 1, 46; Jerome *Letters* 46.14; Vöobus, *History*, 2: p. 365; *H.L.* 6, 40; Soz *H.E.* VI.34; Vöobus, *History*, p. 372.

167. For an alternative vision of choosing and ordaining of presbyters, see Clark, *Building Christian Communities*, pp. 134-145.

Bibliography

The following bibliography has been divided into three sections. The first is a selection of early sources on the ascetic movement. It was chosen to provide a selection of material in English that was relatively accessible and that would give a good sense of the character of the early ascetic movement and of its relationship to the church around it. A very good, complete bibliography of early sources can be found in Chitty, *The Desert a City*. The second section of our bibliography lists the sources that are most helpful for this work. They are works which are, on the whole, contemporary and which either give a good perspective on the nature of the ascetic movement or which actually treat the subject of the article. Even though the literature on the early ascetic movement is considerable, there are very few articles which treat directly the questions of elders and the relationship with the hierarchy of the Church that has been the focus of this book. Those that do, usually take a sacramental or canonical perspective and do not take the specifically pastoral perspective this article has tried to take. Finally, the third section of the bibliography contains works which give a general background. Many of them are helpful for understanding the movement, even though they do not contain material that is immediately helpful for the purpose of this book.

I. Ascetic Writings in English Translations

Ambrose. *Select Works and Letters*. Translated by H. de Romestin. Select Library of the Nicene Fathers, Second Series, vol. 10. New York: The Christian Literature Co., 1896.

Apophthegmata Patrum in *The Paradise of the Holy Fathers*, vol. 2. Translated by E.A.W. Budge. London: Oxford University Press, 1907.

Athanasius. *Select Writings and Letters of Athanasius, Bishop of Alexandria.* Translated by A. Robertson. Select Library of the Nicene Fathers, Second Series, vol. 4. New York: The Christian Literature Co., 1892.

Augustine. *De Moribus Ecclesiae Catholicae.* Translated by R. Stothert. SLNF, vol. 4, 1887.

Expositions on the Book of Psalms. Translated by A.C. Coxe. SLNF, vol. 8, 1888.

Selected Sermons of Augustine. Translated by Quincy Howe. New York: Holt, Rinehart & Winston, 1966.

Basil. *The Ascetic Works of Saint Basil.* Translated by William Kemp Lowther Clarke, D.D. London: Society for Promoting Christian Knowledge, 1925.

Benedict. *The Rule of Saint Benedict in Latin and English.* Translated by Justin McCann. London: Burns Oates, 1952.

Cassian, John. *The Works of John Cassian.* Translated by E. Gibson. SLNF, Second Series, vol. 11. 1894.

Egeria. *Diary of a Pilgrimage.* Translated by George E. Gringras. Ancient Christian Writers, no. 38. New York: Newman Press, 1970.

Etheria (see Egeria).

Eusebius. *The History of the Church.* Translated by G.A. Williamson. Baltimore, Md.: Penguin Books, 1965.

Gregory the Great. *Dialogues.* Translated by O. Zimmerman. FCS, vol. 9, 1952.

The Historia Monachorum in Aegypto in *The Paradise of the*

Holy Fathers. Translated by E.A.W. Budge. vol. 1. London: Oxford University Press, 1907.

Jerome. *The Principal Works of St. Jerome—Letters, Treatises, Prefaces.* Translated by W.H. Fremantle. SLNF, Second Series, vol. 6, 1892.

Jerome and Gennadius. *The Lives of Illustrious Men.* Translated by E. Richardson. SLNF, Second Series, vol. 3, 1892, pp. 349-402.

Palladius. *The Lausiac History.* Translated by Robert T. Meyer. ACW, vol. 34. Westminister, Md.: Newman Press, 1965.

Paulinus of Nola. *Letters.* Translated by P.G. Walsh. ACW, vols. 35-36, 1966.

Possidius. *Vita Augustini.* Translated by H.T. Weiskotten. Princeton: Princeton University Press, 1919.

Sayings of the Fathers. Translated by Sister Benedicta. Oxford: Mowbray, 1975.

Socrates. *The Ecclesiastical History of Socrates Scholasticus.* Translated by S.C. Zenos. SLNF, Second Series, vol. 2, 1890.

Sozomen. *The Ecclesiastical History of Sozomen: A History of the Church from A.D. 323 to A.D. 425.* Translated by C. Hartranft. SLNF, Second Series, vol. 2, 1890.

Sulpicius Severus. *The Life of St. Martin.* Translated by A. Roberts. SLNF, vol. 11, pp. 3-18, 1894.

Theodoret. *The Ecclesiastical History, Dialogues, and Letters of Theodoret.* Translated by B. Jackson. SLNF, Second Series, vol. 3, 1892.

Original Text References:

Butler, Edward C., ed. *The Lausiac History of Palladius.* 2 vols. TSt, vol. 6, 1898/1904.

Cassian. *Iohannis Cassiani: Conlationes XXIII, Institutes Coenobiarium.* Edited by M. Petschenig. CSEL, vols. 13, 17, 1886.

Cotelier, J.B., ed. *Alphabetical Gerontikon* in *Apophthegmata Patrum.* PG, vol. 65, col. 71-440.

Lefort, L. Théophile, ed. *Les vies coptes de Saint Pachôme et de ses premiers successeurs.* Louvain: Bibliothèque du Muséon, vol. 16, 1943, 1966.

Oeuvres de S. Pachôme et de ses Disciples, C.S.C.O. Scr. Copt. tt. 23-24, Louvain, 1956.

S. Pachomii vita bohairica scripta. C.S.C.O. Scr. Copt. ser. 3, t. 7, 1925.

Preuschen, Erwin, ed. *Palladius und Rufinus: Ein Beitrag zur Quellenkunde des Ältesten Mönchtums.* Giessen: J. Richersche Buchhandlung, 1897.

Rosywedus, H., ed. *Verba Seniorum.* PL, vol. 73, col. 355-1022.

II. Directly Helpful Material:

Auf der Maur, I. *Mönchtum und Glaubenserkundigung in den Schriften des S. Johannes Chrysostomus.* Fribourg: Universitäts-Verlag, 1959.

Bacht, Heinrich. "Antonius und Pachomius: Von der Anachorese zum Coenobitentum." *Antonius Magnus Eremita.* SA, vol. 38, Rome: 1956. pp. 66-107.

"Die Rolle des orientalischen Mönchtums in den kirchenpolitischen Auseinandersetzungen um Chalkedon (431-519)," *Das Konzil von Chalkedon.* Edited by Aloys Grillmeier and Henrich Bacht. Würzburg: Echter-Verlag, 1954. pp. 193-314.

"L'importance de l'idéal monastique de S. Pacôme pour

l'histoire du monachisme chrétien." RAM, vol. 26, 1950. pp. 308-326.

"Mönchtum und Kirche. Eine Studie zur Spiritualität des Pachomius," *Sentire Ecclesiam.* Edited by Jean Daniélou and H. Vorgrimler. Fribourg/Berlin: Herder, 1961. pp. 113-133.

"Pakhome et ses disciples," *Théologie de la vie monastique.* Théologie, vol. 49. Paris: Aubier, 1961. pp. 39-71.

Benz, S. "The Monastery as a Christian Assembly," *The American Benedictine Review.* 17. (1966) pp. 166-178.

Bouyer, Louis. *The Meaning of the Monastic Life.* New York: Kenedy, 1955.

Chadwick, Owen. *John Cassian.* Cambridge: University Press, 1950.

Chitty, Derwas J. *The Desert a City.* Oxford: Basil Blackwell, 1966.

Colson, Jean. "Diakon und Bischof in den ersten drei Jahrhunderten der Kirche," *Diaconia in Christo.* Fribourg: Herder, 1962. pp. 23-30.

Croce, Walter. "Aus der Geschichte des Diakonates," *Diaconia in Christo.* Fribourg: Herder, 1962, pp. 92-128.

Daniélou, Jean. "Saint Grégoire dans l'histoire du monachisme," *Théologie de la vie monastique.* Théologie, vol. 49. Paris: Aubier, 1961. pp. 131-141.

DeVogue, Adalbert. *La communauté et l'abbé dans la Regle de Saint Benoît.* Textes et études théologiques. Paris: Desclée de Brouwer, 1964.

"Monachisme et église dans la pensée de Cassien," *Théologie de la vie monastique.* Théologie, vol. 49, Paris: Aubier, 1961. pp. 213-240.

"Le monastère, Église du Christ," *Commentationes in Re-*

gulam S. Benedicti. Ed. by Basilius Steidle. SA. vol. 39. Rome: Herder, 1957. pp. 25-46.

Dorries, H. "The Place of Confession in Ancient Monasticism," *Studia Patristica*, Eng. translation, vol. 5. TU,Vol. 80. Berlin: Akademie Verlag, 1962. pp. 284-311.

Florovsky, Georges. "Empire and Desert: Antinomies of Christian History," *Cross Currents* IX 3, Summer 1959, pp. 233-253.

Gribomont, Jean. "Le monachisme au IVe. S. en Asie Mineure; de Gangres au messalianisme," *Studia Patristica*, vol. 2, TU, Vol. 64. Berlin: Akademie Verlag, 1957. pp. 400-415.

"Le monachisme au sein de L'Église en Syrie et en Cappadoce," *Studia Monastica*, vol. 7. 1965. pp. 7-24.

"Saint Basile," *Théologie de la vie monastique.* Théologie, vol. 49, Paris: Aubier, 1961. pp. 99-113.

Knowles, David. *From Pachomius to Ignatius.* Oxford: Clarendon Press, 1966.

Ladner, Gerhart B. *The Idea of Reform.* Cambridge: Harvard Press, 1959.

Lafontaine, Paul-Henri. *L'évêque d'ordination des religieux.* Ottawa: Les Éditions de l'Université d'Ottawa, 1951.

Leclercq, Jean. "Le sacerdoce des moines," *Irenikon*, vol. 36. 1963, pp. 5-40; Eng. translation in *Monastic Studies*, vol. 3, 1965, pp. 53-86.

"On Monastic Priesthood According to the Ancient Medieval Tradition," *Studia Monastica*, vol. 3, fasc. I, (1961) pp. 137-155.

Leroux, J.M. "Monachisme et communauté chrétienne d'après Saint Jean Chrysostome," *Théologie de la vie monastique.* Théologie, vol. 49. Paris: Aubier, 1961. pp. 143-190.

Morison, Ernest Frederick. *St. Basil and His Rule.* London: H. Froude, 1912.

Mortimer, Robert C. *The Origins of Private Penance in the Western Church.* Oxford: Clarendon Press, 1939.

Munz, Peter. "John Cassian." *Journal of Ecclesiastical History* XI. 1960. pp. 1-22.

Rousseau, O. "Priesthood and Monasticism." *The Sacrament of Holy Orders.* Collegeville, Minn.: Liturgical Press, 1962. pp. 168-181.

Rousseau, P. "The Spiritual Authority of the 'Monk-Bishop': eastern elements in some western hagiography of the fourth and fifth centuries." *Journal of Theological Studies*, n.s. 22 (1971), pp. 380-419.

Steidle, Basilus, ed. *Antonius Magnus Eremita*, Studia Anselmiana, vol. 38. Rome: Herder, 1956.

Tâche, L. "Du moine laïque au religieux prêtre." *Revue de l'Université d'Ottawa.* vol. 2. 1932. pp. 181-210.

Théologie de la vie monastique. Théologie, vol. 49. Paris: Aubier, 1961.

Uedig, Leo. "Die Kanones von Chalkedon in ihrer Bedeutung für Klerus and Mönchtums." *Das Konzil von Chalkedon.* Wurzburg: Echter-Verlag, 1953. pp. 596-676.

Veilleux, Armand. *La liturgie dans le cénobitisme pachômien au quatrième siècle.* Studia Anselmiana. 57, Rome: Herder, 1968. pp. 189-95.

"The Abbatial Office in Coenobitic Life." *Monastic Studies* 6 (1968). pp. 3-46.

Von Severus, E. "Das Monasterium als Kirche," *Enkainia*, ed. H. Emons. Dusseldorf: Patmos-Verlag, 1956.

Vöobus, A. *History of Asceticism in the Syrian Orient.* Vols. 14 & 17. Louvain: CSCO Subsidia, 1958, 1960.

III. Background:

Beck, E. "Asketentum and Mönchtum bei Ephräm." *Il Monachismo Orientale*. Orientalia Christiana Anaclecta, vol. 153. Rome: Pont. Institutum Orientalium Studiorum, 1958. pp. 341-360.

"Ein Beitrag zur Terminologie des ältesten syrischen Mönchtums." *Antonius Magnus Eremita*. Studia Anselmiana. vol. 38. Rome: Herder, 1956. pp. 254-267.

Besse, Jean; Martial, Léon. *Les moines d'Orient antérieurs au Concile de Chalcédoine*. Paris: H. Oudin. pp. 341-430.

Bousset, W. *Apophthegmata: Studien zur Geschichte des ältesten Mönchtums*. Tübingen: Mohr, 1923.

Butler, Edward Cuthbert. *Benedictine Monasticism*. New York: Barnes and Noble, 1961. pp. 293-295.

Chadwick, Owen, ed., *Western Asceticism*. Library of Christian Classics, vol. 12. Philadelphia, 1958.

Colson, J. "Diakon und Bischof in den ersten drei Jahrhunderten der Kirche." *Diaconia in Christo*. Fribourg: Herder, 1962. pp. 23-30.

Festugière, André Jean Marie. *Les Moines d'Orient*. Paris: Éditions du Cerf, 1961.

Folliet, G. "Aux origines de l'ascétisme et du cénobitisme africain." *Saint Martin et son Temps*. Studia Anselmiana. vol. 43. Rome: Herder, 1961. pp. 25-44.

Genier, Raymond. *Les moines et l'église en Palestine au Ve siècle*. Paris: J. Gabalda and Co., 1909.

Gribomont, Jean. *Histoire du texte des ascétiques de S. Basile*. Bibliothèque du Muséon, vol. 32. Louvain: Publications Universitaires, 1953.

Griffe, Élie. "Saint Martin et le Monaschisme gaulois." *Saint Martin et son temps*. Studia Anselmiana. Rome: Herder, 1961. pp. 3-24.

Hamman, Adelbert. *Vie des pères du désert*. Lettres chrétiennes, vol. 4. Paris: Éditions du Cerf, 1961.

Hardy, Edward Rochie. *Christian Egypt: Church and People*. New York: Oxford University Press, 1962.

Heussi, Karl. *Der Ursprung des Mönchtums*. Tübingen: Mohr, 1936.

Holl, Karl. *Enthusiasmus und Bussgewalt in griechischen Mönchtum*. Leipzig: J.C. Hinrichs, 1898.

Hormann, J. *Untersuchungen zur griechischen Laienbeicht*. Donauworth: L. Auer, 1913.

Kemmer, Alfons. *Charisma Maxima: Untersuchung zur Cassians Vollkommenheitslehre*. Louvain: F. Ceuterick, 1938.

Ladeuze, Paulin. *Étude sur le cénobitisme pakômien pendant le IVe siècle et le première moitié du Ve*. Louvain & Paris: J. Van Linthout, 1893, 1962.

Leipoldt, J. *Schenute von Atripe und die Entstehung des national aegyptischen Christentums*. Texte und Untersuchungen, vol. 25. Leipzig: J.C. Hinrichs, 1903.

Louf, A. *The Message of Monastic Spirituality*. New York: Desclee, 1964.

Luff, G. "A Survey of Primitive Monasticism in Central Gaul, 350-700." *The Downside Review* 70 (1952) pp. 180-203.

MacKean, William. *Christian Monasticism in Egypt to the Close of the Fourth Century*. London: Society for Promoting Christian Knowledge, 1920.

Malone, E.E. "The Monk and the Martyr." *Antonius Magnus Eremita*. Studia Anselmiana, vol. 38. Rome: Herder, 1956. pp. 108-135.

Martin, Francis. "Monastic Community and the Summary Statement in Acts," in *Contemplative Community*. Pennington, B. ed. Consortium Press, 1972. pp. 13-46.

McMurry, J. "Poenitentiam agere: A Study of Penance in Monastic-Patristic Writings." *Cistercian Studies*. I, 1966. pp. 74-89.

Merton, T. "Gallo-Roman Monasticism, Cassian, the *Regula Magistri*, and the background to the Rule of St. Benedict." Choir Novitiate conferences. Gethsemani: 1963. (unpublished)

Meyer, L. "Perfection chrétien et vie solitaire dans la pensée S. Jean Chrysostome." *Revue d'ascétique et de mystique* 14 (1933) pp. 232-62.

Pargoire, J. *Les débuts du monachisme a Constantinople*. Revue Quatrième Histoire 65 (1899).

Poschmann, Bernhard. *Penance and the Anointing of the Sick*. New York: Herder and Herder, 1964.

Ryan, John. *Irish Monasticism*. Ithaca: Cornell University Press, 1972.

Schiwietz, S. *Das morganländische Mönchtum*. Tübingen: Mohr, 1936.

Van der Meer, Frederick. *Augustine the Bishop*. Translated by B. Battershaw and G.R. Lamb. London/New York: Sheed & Ward, 1961.

Wagenmann, Julius. *Entwicklungsstufen des altesten Mönchtums*. Tübingen: Mohr, 1929.

Watkins, Oscar Daniel. *A History of Penance*. London: Longmans, Green & Co., 1920.

White, E. *The History of the Monasteries of Nitria and Scetis*. New York: 1933.

Zumkeller, Adolar. *Das Mönchtums des heiligen Augustinus*. Würzburg: Augustinus-Verlag, 1950.